waking to WONDER

100 love letter exchanges with God

MOLLIE AXTELL

CAPTIVATED PRESS
Austin, Texas

Waking to Wonder
Copyright © 2021 Mollie Axtell

Published by Captivated Press
3939 Bee Cave Road C– 100 Austin 78746

www.MollieAxtell.com

No part of this book may be used or reproduced in any manner whatsoever without written permission except in the case of brief quotation embodied in critical articles and reviews.

Scriptures on pages 2, 5, 10, 13, 20, 23, 26, 35, 41, 44, 52, 55, 63, 69, 71, 76, 79, 82, 85, 87, 90, 93, 104, 107, 110, 113, 115, 123, 125, 128, 134, 140, 143, 146, 148, 150, 153, 158, 164, 167, 173, 176, 182, 185, 188, 194, 200, 202, 205, 214, 216, 218, 222, 224, 232, 235, 238, 240, 243, 248, 251, 254, 257, 263, 268, 271, 274, 292, 295, 298, 301, 304, 306, are taken from the Holy Bible, New Living Translation, copyright © 1996, 2004, 2007, 2013, 2015 by Tyndale House Foundation. Used by permission of Tyndale House Publishers, Inc., Carol Stream, Illinois 60188. All rights reserved.

Scriptures on pages 8, 16, 18, 131, 170, 208, 220, 227, 277, 280, 282, 285, 309 taken from the NEW AMERICAN STANDARD BIBLE®, Copyright © 1960, 1962, 1963, 1968, 1971, 1972, 1973, 1975, 1977, 1995 by The Lockman Foundation. Used by permission.

Scripture on pages 32, 38, 47, 49, 98, 101, 260, 290 taken from THE HOLY BIBLE, NEW INTERNATIONAL VERSION®, NIV® Copyright © 1973, 1978, 1984, 2011 by Biblica, Inc.® Used by permission. All rights reserved worldwide.

Scripture quotation on page 161 is from the ESV® Bible (The Holy Bible, English Standard Version®), copyright © 2001 by Crossway, a publishing ministry of Good News Publishers. Used by permission. All rights reserved.

Scripture on page 191 taken from The Message. Copyright Â© 1993, 1994, 1995, 1996, 2000, 2001, 2002. Used by permission of NavPress Publishing Group.

Scriptures on pages 66 and 120 taken from the Holy Bible, New International Reader's Version®, NIrV® Copyright © 1995, 1996, 1998, 2014 by Biblica, Inc.™ Used by permission of Zondervan. www.zondervan.com The "NIrV" and "New International Reader's Version" are trademarks registered in the United States Patent and Trademark Office by Biblica, Inc.™

Scripture quotations on pages 60, 191, 197 are taken from The Living Bible copyright © 1971. Used by permission of Tyndale House Publishers, Carol Stream, Illinois 60188. All rights reserved.

Cover and interior design: Tamara Dever, TLC Book Design,
TLCBookDesign.com

ISBN-Hardcover: 978-1-7360391-0-6 | ISBN-Paperback: 978-1-7360391-1-3

"You will show me the way of life,
granting me the joy of your presence
and the pleasures of living with you forever."
PSALM 16:11

"*Waking to Wonder* will stir your soul to consider a God who is loving, near, and awesome. Mollie Axtell writes with the raw passion of a woman who knows her Savior intimately. This book will encourage you, challenge you, and draw you closer to the God who loves you just as you are, but won't leave you that way."

Michael Blue, author, *Free to Follow*

"I love the way Mollie Axtell writes. She is so personal and real. Her writing encourages you to experience a Heavenly Father who embraces you and loves you. Read this as a daily devotional or incorporate it in your prayers. Either way, you will find comfort and love on each page."

Susan Campbell, author, *A Wild & Wonderful Life*,
founder of More Than You Imagine Ministries

"Mollie Axtell's love letter exchanges sometimes rock me to my very core as my heart aches from her naked emotional honesty. However, the compassionate and loving responses from God to her always give me a sense of his purpose, grace and sovereignty filled with hope and love, as I face my own emotional and physical battles."

Tab Gray, pastor, Family of God Christian Fellowship,
Puerto Peñasco, Mexico

"*Waking to Wonder* reminds us of how greatly loved we are by the Lord of the Universe — our Abba. This book will be on my study table as a guide to come back to what is important… our connection to the Lord and listening to his loving voice."

Nancy Krenek, CEO/founder, R.O.C.K

"Cultivating deep intimacy with God can be extremely difficult in our world today. Through these love letters Mollie is calling us to slow down and wake up to the Wonders of God by allowing our souls to be refreshed in His presence."

Katherine Wolf, author, *Suffer Strong* and *Hope Heals*

"So creative — a wonderful way to express intimate and tender thoughts to and from God! I was immediately drawn to *Waking to Wonder*. Each biblical truth is introduced with a key verse and often a look into the theological concept that is then captured in the love letter that follows. Collectively, the love letters reveal that life with God has many facets, many ups and downs, and many opportunities to not only express our love for God, but also receive the expression of His love for us."

Dr. Buck Anderson, pastor, Leadership Development,
Grace Bible Church College Station, Texas and co-author,
Unlocking Key Biblical Words

"Having the privilege of being Mollie's pastor for years now, I can attest to the reality of what you will discover in this book. Mollie is a life-giver. Spending time with Mollie will leave you spiritually refreshed. I praise God for the encouragement you are about to receive as you read *Waking to Wonder*."

Phil Christensen, pastor, Southwest Bible Church, Austin, Texas

"Mollie's writing infuses hope into my weary heart. With every love letter, there is a powerful draw to the Father through a fresh, honest picture of his incomprehensible love!"

Erin Kiltz, founder and director,
Brookwood in Georgetown

"*Waking to Wonder* invites readers to open a treasure trove of Mollie Axtell's personal conversations with her Creator. Mollie's poignant and relatable love letters to and from God encourage those of us who too often struggle with questions surrounding our identity, self-esteem, and self-image to dig deeper into our relationships with him — instead of our own egos — for the answers."

Lauren Flake, author, artist,
LaurenFlake.com

CONTENTS

TREASURED 1
    Abba's Child 2
    Making a Masterpiece 5
    No Fairy Tale 8
    Fully Known Fully Loved 10
    Treasured 13
    Threadbare Beauty 16
    Child of Promise 18
    Passion to Please 20
    No Strut or Grovel 23
    Currency of Desire 26

SKYWRITING 31
    Extreme Makeover 32
    Diabolical, Delusional, or Divine 35
    Holding the Universe and Me 38
    Skywriting 41
    Marvelous or Maniacal 44
    Worshiping the Giver 47
    Mercy to Breathe 49
    Something From Nothing 52
    Pride in My Glory 55

BRAVE ENOUGH 59
    Courage to Speak 60
    Waiting Well 63
    Brave Enough 66

Soothing My Soul 69
Surprising Superheroes 71

GLIMMER IN THE DARK 75
Obsessed With My Prize 76
Real Life 79
Longing for Light 82
Captive Gaze 85
Relaxing Clenched Fists 87
Neon Lights 90
Glimmer in the Dark 93

LIFE SUPPORT 97
Strong Medicine 98
Better Than Life 101
Life Support 104
Be My Rescue 107
Promise Keeper 110
My Remedy 113
Inseparable 115

SHIFTING SHADOWS & HEAVENLY LIGHTS 119
Fooling Ourselves 120
Read My Lips 123
Shifting Shadows & Heavenly Lights 125
The Art of Remaining 128
A Confident Approach 131
Every Moment of Forever 134

UNBRIDLED BLISS 139
Thunder and Whisper 140

The Party Never Ends 143
Oasis 146
Waking to Wonder 148
See and Be Glad 150
Unbridled Bliss... 153

THE KINDNESS OF CONVICTION **157**
What Are You Drinking? 158
At Home 161
Living Love 164
Power to Cling.. 167
The Kindness of Conviction 170
God's Green Thumb 173
Love Laws 176

EXPOSED THORNS.. **181**
Limping Home 182
Savor the Sip 185
Exposed Thorns 188
Pools of Blessing 191
Swimming With Alligators 194
Life in the Briar Patch 197
Making Monet 200
Was it Because… 202
Defy the Darkness 205
Cracked Clay 208

IN THIS LABYRINTH.. **213**
Seeing Through Doubt 214
Captivated 216
In The Labyrinth 218

Your Road, Reality, and Roots 220
  Overflowing Hope 222
  Honeysuckle on the Wind 224
  One of Those 227

RABBIT HOLES AND REALITY **231**
  Dry Up, Blow Up, or Grow Up 232
  Treasure Trove 235
  Rabbit Holes and Reality 238
  Identity Truth 240
  Wisdom From Above 243

PROMISED TO YOUR PATH **247**
  Prayerful and Proactive 248
  Making Me Rich 251
  Bags of Gold 254
  The Moment He Knocks 257
  Gifts For My Enemies 260
  Promised to Your Path 263

MAKE US ONE **267**
  Strike a Chord 268
  Superfood 271
  Make Us One 274
  Difficult Ones 277
  Ignite Our Souls 280
  Love With Legs 282
  Caught Up In Your Symphony 285

FRAGRANT DAYS **289**
  Unveiled 290

With or Without Words 292
Come On In 295
Deep Roots 298
One Thing 301
Staycation 304
Emerging Love 306
Fragrant Days 309
About the Author..313
Acknowledgments 313
Photo Credits 314

Beloved,

Whether we are suffering or celebrating, I believe each day is an invitation to wake up to the wonder of God. For many years, I made it a practice to write to God about what was on my heart after worshiping and meditating on Scripture. At some point along the way, I started listening to what he might have to say to me in response and writing it down.

After decades of spending time in God's Word, I had a solid foundation to know whether, or not, what I thought I heard was in keeping with Scripture. That was, and always will be, my litmus test.

It never occurred to me to ever let anyone read my love letter exchanges. That felt like revealing something too private and sacred. (Nightmares about showing up to a crowded event not fully dressed came to mind.) I feel very exposed even worshiping in public because it is such an intimate experience for me. Why would I let other people read my vulnerable, raw conversations with God? Sometimes I felt like I was hemorrhaging on the page — not something I desired others to witness.

But God placed a burning desire in my heart to help others cultivate a more passionate devotion to him. Was there a way I could contribute? I thought if I were willing to share something about my connection with God, maybe it would inspire others to connect more deeply with him.

My life has been a montage of extreme peaks and valleys. The phrase in the old Olympic Game's trailer "the thrill of victory and agony of defeat" comes to mind. Over the years, I had several people ask me to write about my life. I declined explaining that memoir would not even make good fiction. My reality did not seem plausible. I was not interested in revealing every tragic detail of my "not fit for prime time" story. I was more interested in writing about how I walked (and sometimes crawled) through it with God and what I learned along the way. At some point, I realized my love letter exchanges with God told that story.

Nine years ago, I began to lead a Celebrate Recovery group. Our worship leader challenged me to write and send out a devotional each week with our group email. I knew with my packed schedule I couldn't originate a devotional every week unless I was willing to share something I was already writing. My love letter exchanges came to mind.

I struggled. Felt resistant. Felt compelled. Agreed. Retracted. Surrendered.

At first, I literally took what I wrote, word for word, in my time with God that morning and posted it, in all its unrefined glory, in the email. (It was like running off the end of the high diving board before I could chicken out.) No points for great form but I was in the water. Once my love letters were out there though, they seemed to be encouraging people.

In retrospect, I would compare it to the feelings I had when my children left for college. Fear, hope, worry and joy all tangled up together. Fortunately, I resisted the temptation to drag them back home to "safety."

Before I go any further, let me be clear. At no time did I ever think these impressions from God were flawless. He is flawless. I am not. I am not pretending to speak perfectly for God. I would encourage you to think of my love letter exchanges as a literary device that really works for me. When I hear God say, "I love you," it impacts me very differently than reading the words "God loves you." Same truth, different delivery. Personalizing the message transforms me.

I hope you will take to heart what is helpful and leave what is not. It is my prayer that something in these exchanges will draw your heart more deeply into the magnificent beauty of our God and you will be refreshed and nourished there.

Bless you,
Mollie

TREASURED

Who does God say I am?

ABBA'S CHILD

"And because we are his children,
God has sent the Spirit of his Son into our hearts,
prompting us to call out, 'Abba, Father.'"
GALATIANS 4:6

My Abba,

Today, when I think of my identity as your child, it stirs up a swarm of memories. Mostly, I am remembering how my husband Cal demonstrated his love for our children. I have vivid memories of how their dad showed his love as he diapered, fed, rocked, carried, and sang lullabies to them (albeit, at times, Jerry Jeff Walker tunes). He showed them his love as he strapped them into car seats and told them adventurous, and painfully corny, bedtime stories.

He corrected them, set boundaries and hugged their adorable, and sometimes, defiant little necks. He wrote one-of-a-kind, comical songs celebrating each of them and played them on his guitar. I loved how they danced, with total abandon, to their songs most every night until they were too cool to do so any longer.

He taught them about relationship with you, encouraged them to enjoy good books, music, art and theater, and showed them how to shoot a basketball. He demonstrated how to work hard, pursue wisdom and integrity, and develop their gifts. Although he was, by no means, perfect like you are, there are some encouraging parallels that come up for me when I reflect on his love for them and your love for me.

It occurs to me that Cal didn't wait until they expressed a need to provide for it. He knew, most times, what they needed way before they did. He didn't wait until they were starving or their toes were cramped in ill-fitting shoes to make the money to feed and clothe them.

Some of his good deeds were not recognized until many years later — or have never been. At times, he did good things for them, even

---

ABBA: *a personal name for father that implies warm affection and devoted trust.*

when they wailed about it. Some of his actions, they instinctively saw as loving. Others, they simply tolerated. They hated a few good things he did. But if it was what he thought was best for them, he did it anyway.

I see more clearly the ways you demonstrate your love for me as I replay these memories. I am also noticing some parallels with my good and bad attitudes, responses and doubts. Before I knew to even think about or whisper a need to you, you provided for me. You have given me life, nurtured, taught, and comforted me.

You have instilled in me a love for your beauty and adventures. You have shown your delight in me and encouraged and empowered my gifts. You have "strapped" me into situations I did not want or understand, while taking me places I had no desire to go. You have held me as I wailed.

You have corrected and disciplined me. You have saved my rebel-self from running off into oblivion. You have taught me how to dance as I sing your love songs. (Thank you that I am still not too cool to dance with you in the kitchen, when no one else is looking.)

Thank you for creating me to know your love. I love being loved by you. Today, your Spirit in my heart prompts me to call out "Abba, Father!"

I love you,
Mollie

My Child,

Although there are limitations to your analogy, it helps for you to have a human illustration of a devoted father's love for his children. Many people have never witnessed this. It grows your perception of my love and your identity as my child. I want my words to carry weight with you. I want you to understand who you are to me, and who you are because of me. As your Father, I want my love to inspire in you "warm affection and devoted trust."

Don't play armchair god, letting your unanswered questions peck at your trust in me. When you don't understand what I have allowed (or not allowed), you can be tempted to pass judgment on me. I promise you cannot run my universe (or your life) better than I can. At times, you shudder at what I am doing, but get some clarity on my impeccable motives years later. Other times, you recognize my actions are grounded in my perfect love. My love for you doesn't fluctuate with your mercurial responses to me.

Let the constancy of my love kindle your trust in me. I will continue to remove what dampens your appreciation of my love for you. I want you to celebrate my fierce, unfailing love for you and treasure each priceless moment as my beloved child. You will always belong to me. I cannot cease to be your Father, and you cannot cease to be my child.

Even when you don't act like you belong to me, you cannot alter your identity as my child. It is who you are. And as my child, you are mine forever.

I love you,
Abba

MAKING A MASTERPIECE

"For we are God's masterpiece. He has created us anew in Christ Jesus, so we can do the good things he planned for us long ago." EPHESIANS 2:10

My Child,

Because of my love for you, I brought you to life, physically and spiritually. Due to the wealth of my favor for you, I offered you the opportunity to become one with Christ. I gave you the greatest gift of all — the gift of a forever life with me.

Now I am chiseling at the rough edges in your life to make you my masterpiece — the beautiful version of you I intended when I created you. Some of your flaws need to fall away completely. Other aspects need a little shaping.

Your traits that reflect me need to be exposed and made more prominent. This involves diminishing what obscures them. I know that is painful sometimes. But it will be worth it. This process allows you to better participate with me in my awesome plans and purposes. The goal is for your heart to become more closely aligned with mine.

You were without hope and help, but now you belong to me. That belonging brings you endless, infinite, beautiful possibility. You are a part of my exquisite living temple I am crafting by expertly joining you together with your brothers and sisters.

I want your life to point others to my perfection. Don't strive to do this. You can only glorify me when you allow me to empower that work in you. I have everything you need and am more than willing to share.

I love you,
Abba

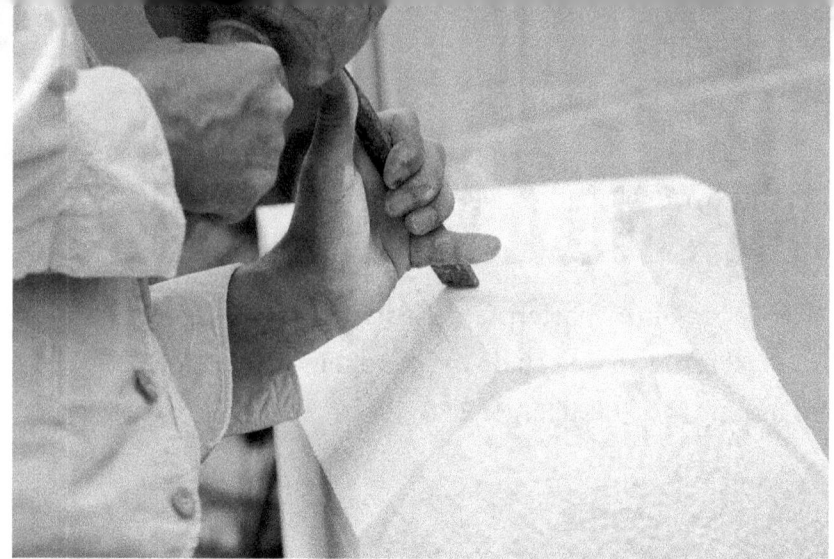

My Abba,

I love that the word translated in this verse as "masterpiece" is the Greek word "poiema" from which we derive our word "poem." I want to be your masterpiece, your poem you create and speak into the world.

When I watched a short film just now on a stone carver's process of creating a masterpiece, I think I gained some insight on your process of creating and refining us. Just as it is with stone carving, working with our soul material is an expensive process. Your work in us can cost us in some ways, but your investment is immeasurable.

Like stone we are not easily malleable and while we are in process, the project may not look worthwhile. The stone carver spoke of needing to be intimately acquainted with the subject to create something beautiful. She described it as hard work with a lot of dust but loved that her creations held a unique place in the world and had permanence.

> *"Smooth my rough edges*
> *with your rich mercy*
> *and tender love"*

I know, at times, it is difficult to refine my features. Those who witness your extravagant efforts to sculpt me might doubt if anything beautiful could ever come from all this sweat and dust. Thank you for being intimately acquainted with me and persistently investing in me, despite how I might look while under construction. Thank you that as one of your creations I have a unique, permanent place in your Kingdom.

Make me the image bearer you want me to be. Uncover the masterpiece you envision. I want to be single-minded, wholly devoted to you, but that is impossible apart from you. I am not up to the challenge of living for your glory without you.

Smooth my rough edges with your rich mercy and tender love today, so I can do the good things you planned for me long ago. Please equip me with everything I need to become your masterpiece — a radiant display of your splendor.

I love you,
Mollie

NO FAIRY TALE

"For we too were once foolish, disobedient, deceived, enslaved to various lusts and pleasures, spending our life in malice and envy, hateful, hating one another. But when the kindness of God our Savior and His love for mankind appeared, He saved us, not on the basis of deeds which we did in righteousness, but in accordance with His mercy, by the washing of regeneration and renewing by the Holy Spirit, whom He richly poured out upon us through Jesus Christ our Savior, so that being justified by His grace we would be made heirs according to the hope of eternal life." TITUS 3:3–7

My Abba,

Thank you so much for entering into relationship with me through your divine provision. Thank you for not leaving me to my own devices. Thank you for reminding me that you loved me when I was foolish, disobedient, deceived, enslaved, envious and hateful.

Not exactly an attractive relationship profile. Especially since you happen to be perfect. I don't think we would be considered an obvious match on one of those dating websites.

Thank you that I did not have to enhance my image and embellish my accomplishments for you to choose me. I am no prize. But you are. You brought everything to the table. I brought nothing. All you ask me to do is accept your offer. What an amazing transaction!

I am imagining my husband telling me about a business arrangement structured in such a one-sided way in his favor. That would be considered an outlandish fairy tale. And yet, you have provided for me in that way.

HEIR: a person legally entitled to the property or rank of another on that person's death, a person inheriting and continuing the legacy of a predecessor

Please continue to press this delightful truth into every crevice of my heart and mind. I want to live as an heir carrying your legacy.

I love you,
Mollie

My Child,

When I adopted you into my family, I made you a rightful heir of living hope and eternal life through Christ's death for your sin. I have given you an unparalleled legacy. I have washed and made you new by my Holy Spirit, whom I poured out generously.

I created you and know you. The real you. The beloved one you don't even fully know yourself. I love you with my flawless, infinite, forever love. I could never base my love on your flaws and assets. I love you whether you are naughty or nice. But now that you have the Holy Spirit to empower you, I don't want you to live in the prison of sin from which I rescued you. I want much more for you than that intolerable survival.

I want you to live each day from my well of living water. I want to pour out my Spirit in you without measure. I am always ready, willing and able to supply everything you need to live this life with me.

Let me renew your heart, mind and body today with my endless love. This is no fairy tale.

I love you,
Abba

FULLY KNOWN FULLY LOVED

"O Lord, you have examined my heart and know everything about me. 4 You know what I am going to say even before I say it, Lord. 13 You made all the delicate, inner parts of my body and knit me together in my mother's womb. 14 Thank you for making me so wonderfully complex! Your workmanship is marvelous—how well I know it. 16 You saw me before I was born. Every day of my life was recorded in your book. Every moment was laid out before a single day had passed." PSALM 139: 1, 4, 13–14, 16

My Child,

I have known you from eternity past. There was never a time when I did not know and love you. I have never wondered what you would think, say or do. I am always perfectly aware of your thoughts, preferences, dreams, desires, strengths and weaknesses.

When you attempt to hide something about yourself, remember your carefully crafted disguises don't conceal your secrets, or anything else from me. It's like when your children were young and used to cover their eyes and say, "You can't see me."

I always see you. I never have, nor ever will, make another you. I revel in your unique design. I was intimately acquainted with every cell of your body before time began. You are my wonderfully complex workmanship. Be whom I created you to be.

Your inadequacies don't shock me. And your honesty does not keep me informed. I know your thoughts before you do. However, telling me what's on your heart grows our relationship.

KNOW: be absolutely certain or sure about something; have developed a relationship with (someone) through spending time with them; be familiar or acquainted with; have personal experience of

Even though it is not breaking news to me, I love when you express your ideas, requests, struggles, and gratitude. I revel in our communion. No matter what else you do, our relationship is what you are created for. Anything that nourishes our connection is magnificent.

I love you,
Abba

My Abba,

I am blown away this morning when I ponder that the One who knows me best, loves me most. The reality of being fully known and fully loved changes everything for me.

I have invested heavily in my image for most of my life. Since I was a child, I embraced the lie that if anyone really knew me, they would find me too sad and damaged to be a desirable spouse, parent, friend, teacher, or leader.

So I became an expert at reading people and giving them what I thought they needed or wanted from me. I sharpened my skills as a shadow dancer, keeping my real girl safely hidden far from the spotlight of reality. For the most part, my distraction worked. People seemed to like my ability to build my life based only on their needs and desires.

> *"the One who knows me best, loves me most"*

Besides you, not many celebrated when I began to heal and grow out of that lopsided way of doing relationship. You gave me the ability to lay down my "unsanctified mercy" for others that was spawned from my pain, not your plans. Thank you that when I give to others from a place of your power, not my lack, I do not atrophy. I flourish.

Please empower me to live a life of radiant gratitude that comes from being perfectly known and perfectly loved.

I love you,
Mollie

TREASURED

"For you are a holy people, who belong to the Lord
your God. Of all the people on earth, the Lord your God
has chosen you to be his own special treasure.
The Lord did not set his heart on you and choose you
because you were more numerous than other nations,
for you were the smallest of all nations! Rather,
it was simply that the Lord loves you ..."
DEUTERONOMY 7:6–8a

My Child,

I treasure you more than all the elegant mountain peaks I have ever fashioned and draped in exquisite winter white. I love you more than centuries of gilded sunrises emerging from the arms of ebony horizons. I value you more than every dazzling constellation I kindled and spun into space.

You are exceptionally precious to me. I designed you for myself and my unique purposes. You belong to me. I chose you to be my own special treasure. I do not lavish my love on you because you are nicer, smarter, holier or better than others. I do it simply because I cherish you. That is the way of perfect love.

At times, I let you go without what you desire to enhance your appetite for my resources and me. In those seasons, I give you an opportunity for deepening trust in me. I want you to remember that you need me. I sometimes show my love by supplying heavenly "manna," when you are acutely aware of your hunger for my rescue. If I never allowed you to get hungry, do you think you would savor the delight of my gifts?

Real life is in me. I want you to lean into my words and presence so that you are supernaturally satisfied. Then when we walk out into

---

SPECIAL: exceptionally precious, belonging specifically to a particular person, designed for a particular person or purpose

the world together to serve others, you will be overflowing with my power and love.

Remember the indescribable satisfaction you feel right now. That is what you can experience every day as you feast on my truth in my presence. When you depend on me for what you need, it reminds you who provides for you. I don't want you to pin your hopes on your own strength and energy.

Every breath you take is a gift from me. I am the one who holds you together. Remember this if you are tempted to believe you built the abundant life you live. The one who treasures you most is always providing for you.

I love you,
Abba

My Abba,

Many times, I don't embrace the truth that I am your special treasure set apart for your plans and purposes. When I look at definitions, it seems like a treasure is something, or someone, deeply loved and highly valued.

As the deep music of these words resonates in my heart, I find myself weeping over my keyboard. Your lavish love takes my breath away. The truth that you value me the way you do is difficult to wrap my heart around.

> *"Your lavish love takes my breath away."*

The world whispers of my insignificance, "You are not accomplished enough, healthy enough, smart enough, young enough, or wealthy enough." I can forget I am infinitely loved and highly valued by the only one with perfect eyesight and a flawless opinion.

When there is hardship in my life, please remind me of how you can use that distress to create a heightened dependence on you. Please remind me that the experience of circumstantial lack in my life does not demonstrate a lack of your love. I know your perfect love cannot wane or be diminished in any way.

Please give me new eyes to see how you treasure me today!

I love you,
Mollie

THREADBARE BEAUTY

"By faith we understand that the world has been created by the word of God so that what is seen has not been made out of things that are visible."
HEBREWS 11:3

My Abba,

You greet me with another eager summer day brimming with possibility. The sunlight illuminates thousands of jade, olive, and emerald leaves as they dance in a gentle breeze outside my window. I see, once again, the beauty you have created by speaking this all into being.

I only have a glimpse of who you are, but I know you are beautiful because what you make is beautiful.

This beauty I see in creation, I also see in the ways you are re-creating others and me. You are bringing new life out of the withered places in our lives. You are magnificent in your power and compassion as you do this work in us.

Thank you that you did not leave us here to work this out on our own. We do not have your resources or abilities. We do not stand a chance of truly re-creating ourselves in our own strength. But if you spoke the universe into being out of nothing, I know you can make awe-inspiring transformation visible in our lives.

This is my paraphrase of Hebrews 11:3 for my life:

By faith I understand that what will be seen in me in the future will not be made out of what is visible right now.

This is encouraging truth. I don't have to see the transformed one, who looks more like you, right now, to know that she is on the way. I look forward to getting to know the "me" I will be. Please continue to re-create me day by day through your glorious power.

I love you,
Mollie

My Child,

I am not limited in any way when I create or re-create. I don't need superior tools or specific materials to create beauty. Every time I re-create a life, it is simply my desire, love and power that bring something new into being.

If you wonder how I can possibly do this, you are probably more focused on the broken fragments of a life, than the skill of the artist. Consider what my hands have already made.

I love to create and re-create. It is my joy to take all the broken pieces of your life and make a beautiful, glistening mosaic, which points to my perfection. I don't want others to have to sift through the wreckage to see me in you. I want my luminous beauty in you to be on display.

I know your soul feels especially threadbare today. Give me all that feels thin and tattered. I will infuse you with light and life. Surrender to me, and my light and life will shine through all the worn places.

I love you,
Abba

CHILD OF PROMISE

"Tell me, you who want to be under law, do you not listen to the Law? For it is written that Abraham had two sons, one by the slave woman and one by the free woman. But the son by the slave woman was born according to the flesh, and the son by the free woman through the promise."

GALATIANS 4:21–23

My Child,

Christ came to earth to buy your freedom. You were an orphan, enslaved to sin. But I wanted to give you a place in my forever family. You could not initiate your own adoption. That task was in my hands. I am holy — perfectly whole, without flaw. Despite your deficiencies and weaknesses, when you accepted Christ's gift of his life, you were made holy and wholly mine.

Sometimes, though, you feel malnourished because you forget the things of this world are empty and useless to satisfy the famine in your soul. They will just leave a dead taste in your mouth and a swelling hunger in your heart.

I can nourish you ... today and forever.

Don't try to earn favor with me by keeping the rules. You are not a child of the law but a child of my divine promise. I want you to follow me because we love each other and are family. All my thoughts, plans, words and actions are perfect. Follow me because I am your perfect Father. You can trust what I say and do, because it is impossible for me to mess up.

Abraham had two sons, one with his slave and one with his wife. The son of the slave was born in an attempt to force the consummation of what was wanted. But the son of his wife was born as the fulfillment of my promise.

You are a child of the promise, just like Isaac. Don't live like Ishmael, the child born by human effort. Live like Isaac, the child born by the power of my Spirit. That is who you are.

I love you,
Abba

My Abba,

How absurd it is to subsist like a deprived orphan when I am a child of the King of Kings. I don't want to ever walk through my day like an unloved vagabond. By birthright, I know that is not who I am.

I want to experience the privilege of my position in your family. I want to savor every spiritual blessing at your banquet table. I want to bask in the beauty of your presence and the richness of your love.

I long to be a child who sees, listens, and speaks in a way that reminds others I belong to you. I want people in my life to notice a family resemblance.

Please help me to see others more the way you see them. I know if I am walking this path with you, day by day, I will take on more of your characteristics. I am impacted by the company I keep.

Please empower me by your Spirit to live in an obedience to you that is born of our love.

I love you,
Mollie

PASSION TO PLEASE

"You are worthy, O Lord our God, to receive glory and honor and power. For you created all things, and they exist because you created what you pleased." REVELATION 4:11

"Finally, dear brothers and sisters, we urge you in the name of the Lord Jesus to live in a way that pleases God, as we have taught you. You live this way already, and we encourage you to do so even more." 1 THESSALONIANS 4:1

My Abba,

This morning I want to meditate on the reality that you created me for your pleasure. Sometimes it is hard for me to grasp the truth that you fashioned me to please you. I want to give you a reason to rejoice in me as I walk through this day. I want you to enjoy me. I want to do what you created me to do — bring you pleasure.

I have spent much of my life trying to please people. I stretched, bent, and twisted myself into what I thought would make someone else happy. Unfortunately, I was trying to become someone who was not very much like the "me" you made me to be. It has not been rewarding to live like that. Thank you for the ways you are sanctifying my desire to please.

I realize I am eternally pleasing to you because I trusted Christ to restore me to right relationship with you. Thank you that you made a way for my displeasing attitudes and actions to not be counted against me — forever. But I, also, want to live to please you today.

When I look at other verses, I see you give me the desire and power to please you. I am relieved to not feel pressured to please you in my own strength. Thank you for the "want-to" and the "how-to."

PLEASURE: a feeling of happy satisfaction and enjoyment
PLEASE: to cause to feel happy and satisfied

I loved each one of my children, unconditionally, before they drew their first breath. But beyond that, there are things they do that give me pleasure as a parent. I realize I experience joy or pleasure when they:

- Pursue relationship with you
- Love and serve others well
- Walk in their design
- Grow stronger spiritually, emotionally, mentally, and physically
- Make healthy choices

Perhaps that gives me some insight into what gives you, my heavenly Father, pleasure. Please transform me. Give me an increasing passion to please you.

I love you,
Mollie

My Child,

Your experience as a parent does give you some perspective on what gives me pleasure as your Father. When you want to be with me, it brings me joy. When you love those in your life with my unconditional love, I rejoice.

When you become more like me, it brings me pleasure. I enjoy seeing you live in the purpose for which I designed you. When you choose what is good and right, it makes my heart sing.

Together, we can enjoy the life for which I created you. I am not like the people in your life who want you to twist and bend for their latest whim. I am pleased when you are true to whom I have made you to be.

For all eternity past and future, I have never made, nor will ever make, someone exactly like you. You are not rare or uncommon. You are a singular masterpiece. Each of my children is one-of-a-kind. I breathed into being one very distinctive, forever you. Let me show you the path to being uniquely, beautifully you — for my pleasure and my glory!

I love you,
Abba

NO STRUT OR GROVEL

"For those who exalt themselves will be humbled, and those who humble themselves will be exalted."
LUKE 14:11

My Abba,

I realize that sometimes I don't practice humility. I don't hold a truthful opinion of myself. My beliefs don't agree with reality. I may feel like I have failed, when I have succeeded. Or I may feel successful, when I have failed. I react in different ways when I am not in agreement with the reality of who you say I am. I may try to make myself appear more (or less) important.

When I succumb to a false view of myself, my self-esteem can shrink into something frail and ant-like, striving for recognition of my own significance. Or, I may play with false humility. When that happens, I can babble about how flawed I am as a subconscious, or conscious, tactic for gaining affirmation. These are definitely times when I am not listening to you and your truth.

When I feel secure in whom you made me to be, I don't try to disparage myself, or push the parade of my importance. I can sit in the least prestigious spot at the table and feel content in my own skin, because I don't feel invested in promoting my significance. Perhaps then, I have your view of humility.

I want to have a right view of my worth — a truthful opinion of myself. Please silence the other voices and saturate my heart with your flawless view of me.

I love you,
Mollie

HUMBLE : to have a truthful opinion of one's self
EXALT: to raise to a higher rank or a position of greater power
WORTHY: deserving effort, attention, or respect

My Child,

You have several faulty strategies for relieving the pain of feeling unworthy. But no matter to what you resort, my opinion of you is the cure.

Our enemy and the world lie to you about your value. They tell you your value is based on your performance. Hollow accomplishments are touted as paramount. What is eternally important is demeaned. But whose opinion of you matters more than mine? I created you and am re-creating you each day as you surrender to me. Because I am your Creator and Re-Creator, I am the only one who has the right to tell you who you are. You are valuable because what I create is priceless.

> *"I am the only one who has the right to tell you who you are."*

Because you belong to me, you are worthy of all my good gifts. You don't have to make yourself righteous enough to receive from me. You could not, so I have accomplished that for you through your relationship with my Son. You get off-track when you allow others to define you. Don't perform for the approval of humans. They are fickle and, even on their best days, unable to assess you flawlessly.

You are my beloved child. Embrace how unconditionally and perfectly I love you. The more you allow me to wrap you warm in my love, the more you will embrace who you truly are.

No need to strut or grovel. Because I created you in my image and love you, I guarantee you are worthy — deserving effort, attention, and respect. Through me, you can be steadfastly secure in the truth of who I say you are.

I love you,
Abba

CURRENCY OF DESIRE

"In the wilderness their desires ran wild, testing God's patience in that dry wasteland." PSALM 106:14

"Take delight in the Lord, and he will give you your heart's desires." PSALM 37:4

"And the Spirit gives us desires that are the opposite of what the sinful nature desires." GALATIANS 5:17b

"You won't spend the rest of your lives chasing your own desires, but you will be anxious to do the will of God." 1 PETER 4:2

My Abba,

It has taken me countless years and deep healing to begin to recognize my desire. In the midst of abuse as a child, I only knew how to read the desires of others and try to react in a way to minimize pain.

With increasing freedom, I now realize I have my own desires. But I need your wisdom to know what to do with them. I hear opinions from others that range from, "All our desires are good" to "All our desires are evil." But as I look at Scripture, I don't get the sense that you see all our desire as good or bad.

I need your strength to sift through my wants and still pursue what you want. Please show me where the gold is amidst the dross in my desire. How do I acknowledge my desire but not make it my god? I don't want to worship whatever my flesh thinks it wants. At times, my desires can change as quickly as my fickle cravings for peculiar foods did when I was pregnant.

My sin nature is never satisfied for very long marching to the beat of its own erratic drum. It is always on the move looking for that next something to fuel the furnace of my capricious appetites. My desires

can be headstrong and rowdy offspring with great vigor and decent intentions, but at times, not yet mature. I don't want them to run wild. I need you to show me what is inspired by you and what is not. Please sanctify my desires.

I love you,
Mollie

My Child,

I am glad you have come to a place where you more clearly recognize your desire and can choose to bring it to me. In the past, you could not surrender what you did not know was yours.

If you had a bank account that you did not realize was yours, you would not wrestle with how to spend the money in it. There would be no potential for spending it poorly or well, if you didn't know it existed. But if you know you have that resource, you can then choose what to do with it. That is how it is with the currency of desire. When you realize you have it, you then can decide how to spend it.

> *"Your desire can come into beautiful alignment with mine to spawn something remarkable."*

Your desire is not always wrong. Sometimes it is what makes you uniquely you. I want you to shine for me in your singular way. I made you the way you are for a reason. But your sinful nature can taint the divine desire I have placed in you. Bring it to me, so I can help you sort it out.

Your desire can come into beautiful alignment with mine to spawn something remarkable. I can infuse your heart with what is right, good and a priority in my kingdom. I know you want to commit to the path that aligns your heart with mine. And as your desires merge with mine, your soul will be supernaturally satisfied.

I love you,
Abba

SKYWRITING
What is God Like?

I love you

EXTREME MAKEOVER

"When Jesus spoke again to the people, he said, 'I am the light of the world. Whoever follows me will never walk in darkness, but will have the light of life.'"
JOHN 8:12

My Child,

I stimulate sight and make things visible. My light does not discriminate between the good, the bad, the lovely and the unlovely.

When I light up the home of your heart, I don't only shine on the areas that are functional, orderly, and well swept. I also shine on the broken plumbing, water stains, and leaking roof.

> *"You need a professional.*
> *I excel at renovation."*

My holy light reveals all things. That is why you need my supernatural mercy and grace. The rooms of your heart are works in progress needing my extreme makeover. Just when you get the repairs in one room "under control," you notice the drastic need for a remodel in another.

You need a professional. I excel at renovation. On your own, you will wind up exhausted and discouraged. You need my power and skills to make true and lasting change. I reveal what needs my touch, so you can be transformed.

Follow me and treasure my light, no matter what it uncovers. Give me those unsightly defects that became visible to you when we opened that wall. I knew about them already. Your broken bits cannot surprise

---

LIGHT: an agent that stimulates sight and makes things visible

me. And, I am perfectly equipped to take care of those places in the worst disrepair.

I am your Light and your Healer. I can make the wrong things right.

I love you,
Abba

My Abba,

Thank you for making your home in my heart. As you illuminate my heart, I will trust you to show me what's in need of repair. I don't want to wander around in the dark with my little flashlight trying to fix what is damaged.

Unless I am led by you, the Light of the World, I will chase shadows. Thank you that there is no darkness in you.

I like the idea of my heart as a home you are renovating. I pray as I move through today, you would remind me who has the power tools and can do the heavy lifting. That would not be me. Please give me the supernatural ability to walk in humility deferring to the One with infinite knowledge, strength, and grace.

Please give me confidence in your blueprints. Sometimes I think I have a better plan. Forgive me. Show me what needs your attention today. Show me when you want me to pick up a hammer and participate. Show me when to be still and wait, as you work.

Make my heart tender and sensitive to your Spirit. I want to be encouraged by the progress you have made in me, even when my view is obscured by the rubble that is part of any building project.

So I don't lose heart along the way, please share your vision for my "before and after" as you build your beauty in me.

I love you,
Mollie

DIABOLICAL, DELUSIONAL, OR DIVINE

"For Jesus is the one referred to in the Scriptures, where it says, 'The stone that you builders rejected has now become the cornerstone.' There is salvation in no one else! There is no other name in all of heaven for people to call on to save them."
ACTS 4: 11–12

My Abba,

Scriptures like this one don't leave much philosophical wiggle room. It occurs to me again that Jesus was absolutely diabolical, delusional, or divine.

Either, he was evil incarnate with full awareness that he was asking people to sacrifice themselves for a lie. Or he was a stark raving madman with no grasp of reality. Or he was telling the truth about who he was. Since nothing else in his life screams monstrous or bonkers, the evidence supports the reality that he is God, and what he said is true.

So here is my issue. I am awkward and flustered when I talk about you in the presence of those who don't have any interest in you, find the idea of you a fond fantasy, or even dangerous snake oil. I sense the ill-fitting skates of my self-esteem scuffing around on the pitted ice of our culture.

I feel secure when I am up front speaking to a group of people who are not confronting me. I speak. They don't. There is that protective moat of civility that flows between the crowd and me. But when it is a

casual conversation between a few people, I don't feel the freedom to talk about you in the same way. I think I want you, and my ideas about you, to be liked.

Please forgive me for the times I have dishonored you by trying to please people. I don't want the soot of my sin to obscure "the Way, the Truth, and the Life." Please give me the courage to speak the truth about you in love, no matter what the context or who is present.

I love you,
Mollie

My Child,

You want to avoid conflict and disapproval. You don't deny me. But in certain instances, you try to dress me in trendy camouflage and tuck me in your handbag.

You want to disguise me so they might find me easier on the eyes, more affable, and manageable. I am infinitely too big and wild to fit in the tiny niches where people prop up their other "gods."

Phrases like "no one else" and "no other name" chafe the egos of many people. But what is my choice? Should I tell lies about myself, so I can validate the fickle currents of humanity's wayward tide? My love does not eradicate what is right and wrong. And humans don't get to make up the rules along the way.

I will only speak truth. And many times, people won't like it. So it follows, if you speak truth about me, the majority of people won't like the message or the messenger either. You need to accept that my truth will not make you popular. It blows minds, constructs, and plans. Most people are not fond of relinquishing the ideological skyscrapers they have erected for themselves.

> *"I will give you the words and ways to be an overflowing channel of my magnificent grace."*

Plunge into my glorious presence today! I will give you the words and ways to be an overflowing channel of my magnificent grace. I offer my grace to those who long to immerse themselves in it and to those who may still want to sit on the shore.

I love you,
Abba

HOLDING THE UNIVERSE AND ME

"Do you not know? Have you not heard? The Lord is the everlasting God, the Creator of the ends of the earth, He will not grow tired or weary and his understanding no one can fathom." ISAIAH 40:28

"for the Lord searches every heart, and understands every desire and every thought." 1 CHRONICLES 28:9b

"'I am the Alpha and the Omega,' says the Lord God, 'who is and who was, and who is to come, The Almighty.'" REVELATION 1:8

"because God has said, 'Never will I leave you; never will I forsake you.'" HEBREWS 13:5a

My Child,

I have no beginning or end. I have not just been around a long time. I am timeless. I am not seriously old. I am everlasting.

I spoke all of creation into being. I made everything beautiful that exists from nothing. I hold the universe together. I am not just extremely strong. I am infinitely powerful. Omnipotent.

I have an infinite capacity for what is good. I don't get tired of your needs, concerns and problems and run out of gas. I have endless love, patience, energy and endurance. I am perfectly faithful.

I have infinite understanding. I am not just exceptionally smart. I know everything. I know everything you have done, or will ever do, and all your thoughts. I also know the motives behind your thoughts. Don't worry. There is not some hidden failure that will

surprise me and cause me to jump ship. I know you perfectly and love you completely.

You don't have a problem I need to read up on before I can help. I have seen it all and have all the solutions. I am your beautiful Remedy. I know what brings you life, today and always.

I love you,
Abba

My Abba,

Please give me a truer view of you. I know my mind cannot even begin to fathom your infinite, perfect qualities. But until I see you face to face, I want to grow each day in my awareness of who you are.

Please forgive me when I seek your hand more than your heart. I realize nothing you can give me will rival the gift of your presence in my life. When I am reveling in communion with you, my heart is never more joyfully alive.

Thank you for never losing patience with my juvenile escapades. Thank you for not becoming annoyed with my pocket-sized needs and wants. I am so glad you have an endless ability to care for the tiny and mammoth struggles in my life.

Your capacity for connection is infinite, yet intimate. You have never made me feel like your dance card is too full with commitments to really important people. Thank you that I am never relegated to a folding chair on the fringe of the room while you dance with someone who follows your lead better than I do.

My most minuscule request does not go unnoticed because millions of other people need your attention. That is one of the awesome things about being infinite. You are never too busy, overwhelmed with life, or otherwise preoccupied with the slightly ginormous obligations of running the universe.

Thank you that your flawless attention to, and love for, me will never diminish or go stale. There is no expiration date on your affection. My God who sustains the universe and holds my hand, renew me with your endlessly stunning presence today.

I love you,
Mollie

SKYWRITING

"They know the truth about God because he has made it obvious to them. For ever since the world was created, people have seen the earth and sky. Through everything God made, they can clearly see his invisible qualities—his eternal power and divine nature. So they have no excuse for not knowing God. Yes, they knew God, but they wouldn't worship him as God or even give him thanks. And they began to think up foolish ideas of what God was like. As a result, their minds became dark and confused." ROMANS 1:19–21

My Child,

Since I created humanity, I have used creation to reveal myself to those I created. I want everyone to experience me through the beauty of what they can see in my handiwork. The vibrant stars I sprinkle into the black bowl of a midnight sky. Powder blue waves waltzing across ivory sand. The blaze of the sun dazzling the sable horizon at daybreak. I want my invisible qualities — my power and divine nature — to be made more tangible through these glorious displays of my splendor.

Relationship with me is what all people were created for. The problem is this: despite the ways I reveal myself, many refuse to treat me as God. They even concoct foolish imaginations about what I am like. Because of this, their minds become dark and confused.

They think they are profoundly wise, but they have become foolish. Instead of worshiping me, the one true infinite, glorious, perfect God, they give their deepest devotion and admiration to created things. I do not force them to stop this. I allow them to pursue what their hearts desire. I always give them a choice. Love requires choice. But as a result, some completely turn from the truth about me and invest themselves in lies.

Although I deserve their love and worship as their Creator, they devote themselves to what I created for them to enjoy. They tumble head over heels into deception and reap more and more darkness. This breaks my heart.

Now let's talk about you. I want you to understand that it makes me sad when you choose other things over the life you can find in me.

You make an idol for yourself (or of yourself) whenever you buy the lie that something, or someone, other than me, is worthy of the highest place in your heart. I don't want to see you hurt, disappointed, and broken by your poor choices. Choose to worship me alone. I am never a poor choice. I am worthy of your endless adoration.

I love you,
Abba

My Abba,

After all these years of relationship with you, how do I still get things upside down? I want to be immune from this inversion of priorities. Please help me. Make me increasingly sensitive to your truth.

The more I, and others, go down the twisted road of deception, the darker it gets. Lies can be attired masterfully as beguiling, compelling truth. What is significant to you becomes trivial. What is trivial becomes our passion. Lifeless things can seem worthy of our utter devotion.

"write your words of life across my sky"

I want a heart that breaks with what breaks your heart. I want a heart that rejoices with what brings you joy. I want your priorities. Your passions.

Now, I am imagining those airplanes that write messages in the sky. That is what I desire for you to do each day. Please write your words of life across my sky.

Give me your gift of sight. I want to recognize and appreciate you as my God — first and foremost in my life. Then everything, and everyone, else will take their rightful place in my heart.

I love you,
Mollie

MARVELOUS OR MANIACAL

"Great and marvelous are your works, O Lord God, the Almighty. Just and true are your ways, O King of the nations. Who will not fear you, Lord, and glorify your name? For you alone are holy. All nations will come and worship before you, for your righteous deeds have been revealed." REVELATION 15:3–4

My Abba,

You have shown me who you are through many great and marvelous works. I am so grateful you have allowed me to see firsthand your magnificent transformation in the lives of so many people, including me. Your righteous deeds have been revealed.

I have seen you take people who are unable to even articulate their pain and transform them into vibrant witnesses to your grace. I have seen you restore marriages and families. I have seen you supernaturally turn the deepest wounds into radiant displays of your splendor.

You are marvelous and what you do is marvelous. You are just and true. And you alone are holy.

So here is my question: If you are marvelous, just, true, and holy, why do so many of us point to injustice in our world and accuse you of being inept, impotent, evil, or non-existent? There is a lot of talk today about not judging other people. But we seem quite anxious to judge you. We constantly sling our arrows of accusation into the heavens.

If you are not perfect, you have been selling us a lie. Either you are flawed, dishonest, and not worthy of anyone's worship. Or, you are utterly worthy of our worship and falsely accused by many of those you created. I see it cannot be both ways.

When I look at creation as a whole, the life of Christ, and the supernatural ways you work, it does not support the idea that you

are some kind of man-made god with broken limbs who has toppled under the weight of our false expectations.

You have revealed your character to me for decades, and I know you are flawless. You are just and true. You cannot act unjustly. So why do we rail against you, accusing you of gross negligence (at best), when something happens that we perceive to be unjust?

I guess you are the most convenient place to dispatch blame. You are definitely a massive target, since you are in-charge of our universe. Please forgive me for the times I have misread your intentions. Many times I don't understand why you allow the pain.

When I become the red-faced, brokenhearted toddler with swollen eyes wailing because I can't understand your parenting style, please give me the ability to trust in your unwavering love.

I love you,
Mollie

My Child,

I made human understanding to be pretty powerful, but it is still limited. Those I created desire for me to enter into every situation and bring the outcome they think they want, even though their perceived sense of justice and desire can shift quickly.

Sometimes, humans can "look down" on me as they play cosmic judge and jury to determine if they think I have dictated circumstances according to their standards. If I have not run interference in the way they want me to, they blame me for not providing the desired outcome.

I know you can become overwhelmed by your pain and don't fully understand my ways. There is a higher price to freewill than you can imagine. You don't have the million-mile view like I do.

Please give me what you perceive to be the most horrific of circumstances. Lay all that suffering at my feet. I can bring beauty from ashes. I will not always make life pain-free. But I can redeem any hurt. I can transform the severely wounded ones into instruments of my glory.

I am worthy of all your worship, even when you feel like you are drowning in the "whys" of life.

I love you,
Abba

WORSHIPING THE GIVER

"They exchanged the truth about God for a lie, and worshiped and served created things rather than the Creator — who is forever praised. Amen."
ROMANS 1:25

My Abba,

I usually think of this passage as referring to people who don't have a relationship with you, at all. But when I look at these two definitions, I see I may be looking too far from home. I can be guilty of worshiping created things instead of you, the Creator of all.

I show what I worship by the way I set my priorities. What takes precedence? What consumes my thoughts? To what do I give myself? For what, or whom, will I sacrifice?

At times, I allow people, possessions, accomplishments or entertainment to become my priority. I realize those priorities can be positive until they take precedence over you and consume my thoughts, time and energy. Then I give myself to them in a way that is inappropriate and depleting. Please forgive me.

When I elevate something, or someone, above you in my heart, I am engaging in false worship. But in that moment, I am deceived. I don't call it what it is. Please transform me.

I want your gifts to continually lead me to you, the Giver. I don't want to be like the spoiled child on Christmas who won't come to the dinner table to spend time with the family who gave her gifts, because she is obsessed with the new toys under the tree. Please set me free from the worship of anything, or anyone, else but you.

I love you,
Mollie

WORSHIP: *to show reverence and adoration for God; to treat (someone or something) with the reverence and adoration appropriate to God*

My Child,

Your Christmas analogy is a good place to begin. Christmas is meant as a celebration of Christ. But it has been distorted. Instead of focusing on the greatest gift of all — Christ coming to mankind — the swapping of gifts between friends and family is lifted up above this glorious reality.

The created is worshiped above the Creator. The gifts are center stage. The Giver is forgotten.

This is a good picture of the propensity of people to do this every day. Our enemy will attempt to cement your heart to any gift that distracts you from me. I want you to be more alert to this insidious strategy that can hijack your heart.

You were created to receive from me. I desire for you to be thankful for the gifts I give. But I want them to point you to me. Otherwise, the very gifts I give you will become idols — lifeless things that you have lifted above me in your heart.

We can enjoy the good things in your life together. I designed you for that pleasure. Stay close to me as you indulge in the lavish blessings I will share with you today. The gifts I give are displays of my splendor. I can show you the best ways to enjoy them — for your good and my glory.

I love you,
Abba

MERCY TO BREATHE

"Therefore, since we have a great high priest who has ascended into heaven, Jesus the Son of God, let us hold firmly to the faith we profess. For we do not have a high priest who is unable to empathize with our weaknesses, but we have one who has been tempted in every way, just as we are—yet he did not sin.
Let us then approach God's throne of grace with confidence, so that we may receive mercy and find grace to help us in our time of need." HEBREWS 4:14–16

My Child,

My flawless compassion gives me the desire to relieve your suffering. But I went further than just entertaining a strong feeling, or wishing things could be different for you.

Through my Son, I poured my deity into the helpless form of a human infant. He was born into a time and place where people immediately wanted to murder him. There are many postcard-worthy, idyllic spots in my creation where we could have staged a magnificent entrance. But my Son spent his first days in a cattle trough. A little-noticed miracle in a manger! (Not, in any way, as peaceful as it looks in the paintings.)

His mother was a blessed but frightened, inexperienced girl who had very little idea what she was getting into. I interrupted perfect, joy-filled, eternal communion in the Trinity for those inglorious beginnings in a stable complete with manure and dirty animals. There was no Twitter feed to announce his celebrity arrival. No headlines proclaiming, "Today God Became Human!"

MERCY: compassion or forgiveness shown toward someone whom it is within one's power to punish or harm, performed out of a desire to relieve suffering   COMPASSION: concern for the suffering of others   LATIN: compati 'suffer with'

And as it turned out, these extraordinarily humble beginnings were not going to be the most challenging chapter in his earth story. Until the triumph of his resurrection, he experienced immense spiritual, emotional and physical adversity.

I am heavily invested in this living, breathing connection with you. I know how you struggle. I understand because I have truly taken on skin and shared in the stress and strain of being human.

You can come confidently to me. I have made a way through Christ's life, death and resurrection. Because you have accepted his sacrificial gift, you can come to my throne of grace and find everything you need.

I love you,
Abba

My Abba,

Thank you that you can sympathize with my weakness. Thank you for choosing a hands-on experience with this world and its trials and temptations. You do not sit back lounging on some cushy cloud recliner uninformed about how hard it is to live in this world.

You have been here and done this. You understand how challenging it can be to thrive in a place where our enemy is hell-bent on using us for target practice. Thank you that despite his hostilities, you are ultimately victorious and made provision for us to always approach you with confidence. Not confidence in what we have, or have not, done. But utter confidence in what you have done perfectly for us.

> *"Thank you that the gateway to our relationship is not about my performance, but your perfection."*

You provide pure rest. Thank you that I don't have to stress about measuring up. Thank you that the gateway to our relationship is not about my performance, but your perfection. And thank you that in your presence, I find the mercy and grace I need to breathe.

I love you,
Mollie

SOMETHING FROM NOTHING

"Standing nearby were six stone water jars, used for Jewish ceremonial washing. Each could hold twenty to thirty gallons. Jesus told the servants, 'Fill the jars with water.' When the jars had been filled, he said, 'Now dip some out, and take it to the master of ceremonies.' So the servants followed his instructions. When the master of ceremonies tasted the water that was now wine, not knowing where it had come from (though, of course, the servants knew), he called the bridegroom over. 'A host always serves the best wine first,' he said. 'Then, when everyone has had a lot to drink, he brings out the less expensive wine. But you have kept the best until now!' This miraculous sign at Cana in Galilee was the first time Jesus revealed his glory. And his disciples believed in him."
JOHN 2:6–11

My Child,

I am all about creating something from nothing. I can take the dying embers of your life and fan the flame into something powerful and magnificent. Don't be discouraged by what you see. I am the God of the unseen. I don't need the right intellect, talent, strength, and resources to accomplish my plans and purposes.

Give yourself to me each day and I will create beauty from your lack. You have heard it said I don't give you more than you can handle. That isn't always true. If your life never brings you more than you can handle, why would you ever need me? Sometimes, I do give you much more than you can handle on your own.

But it is never more than I can handle. I can provide you with everything you need to thrive in all your circumstances by the power of my Spirit. Ask me into your deepest place of need today. I breathed galaxies into being. I can carry your pain. Exhale your disappointment. Inhale my comfort. Let my joy be your strength.

I love you,
Abba

My Abba,

At times I feel trapped in the flesh of this temporal tent, a weary vagabond wandering aimlessly from sunrise to sunset. But then you break into my earth-bound routine and bring your glorious, delightful, miraculous presence.

You transform my unremarkable trek into something nascent and full of wonder. You bring joy into my despair. You bring plenty into my lack. You bring your glory to the ceremony of life. You turn my water into wine!

Sometimes I listen for your voice and follow you. Other times, I remain fettered in daily duty, struggle, and the tyranny of the urgent. But you go before me, and come behind me, to create something luminous from the dust of this journey. Circumstances that seem so dark are transformed by your supernatural touch.

*"You bring your glory
to the ceremony of life.
You turn my water into wine!"*

As I get older, I love the phrase, "But you have kept the best until now!" When I meditate on this truth, it seems much deeper than a reference to good wine at a party. It seems like a principle to live by that keeps me from pining at the rearview mirror of my past. I am encouraged to celebrate your beautiful "now."

Enjoying you in this moment is the pinnacle of what you have for me on this earth. If I walk in that reality, the shadows of my past and the fantasies of my future are dethroned. I long to be increasingly sensitized to your Spirit, to partner with you in some small way each day. That is when I truly feel alive.

I love you,
Mollie

PRIDE IN MY GLORY

"But you, O Lord, are a shield around me;
you are my glory, the one who holds my head high." PSALM 3:3

My Abba,

You are my only eternal protection. I realize you don't always intervene on my behalf to free me from all peril on my journey. But I am certain I would not take my next breath without your protection. I have seen enough evil in my life to know that you are pushing back against the darkness that desires to steal, kill and destroy us or we would cease to exist. Thank you for all that you do to protect me emotionally, spiritually, mentally and physically.

I find it interesting that there are so many definitions for the word "glory." But the ones below seem most appropriate to me in this context. You are my magnificence — my great beauty. You are my ultimate cause for pride, respect and delight. You are the source of my greatest pleasure. You are my glory!

It occurs to me that I have always thought of pride in a negative sense. I have only thought of it as a word meaning that I am focused on my own achievements without giving you credit. In the past, I narrowed the definition of "pride" to "arrogance," claiming something for myself that belonged to you. But the definition on the previous page brings new clarity on experiencing pride in you.

I can experience deep pleasure derived from your achievements because I am "closely associated" with you. This reminds me of how kids who love their fathers sometimes feel proud and brag on the things they think make their fathers great. I recall my daughter

---

GLORY: magnificence; great beauty, a thing that is beautiful or distinctive; a special cause for pride, respect, or delight   PRIDE: a feeling or deep pleasure derived from one's own achievements or the achievements of those with whom one is closely associated   ARROGANCE: having or revealing an exaggerated sense of one's own importance or abilities, from Latin arrogant: claiming for oneself

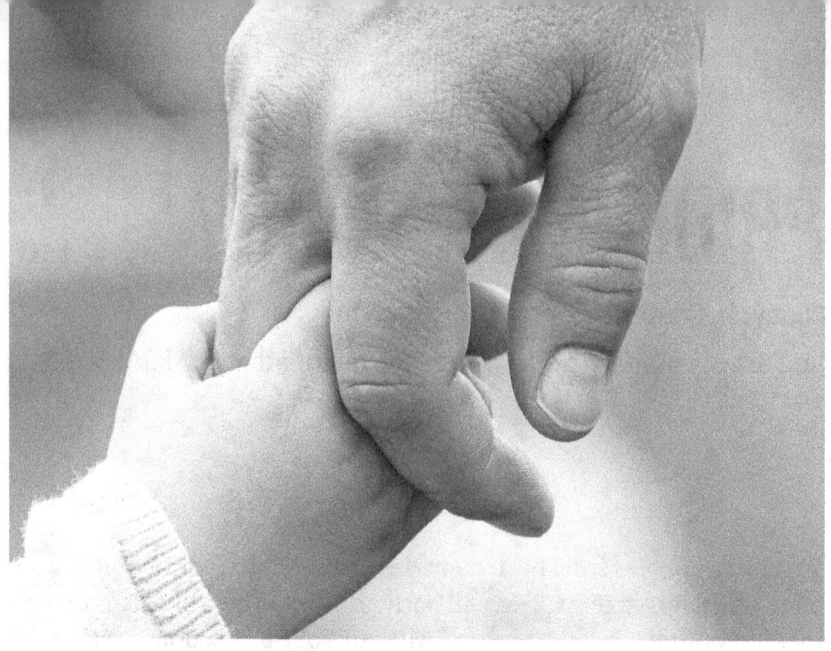

recently telling me what was wonderful about her dad. There were so many things from her father's way of affirming her to their Mexican food and ice cream dates, from the corny songs he sang to the passion for books he instilled in her.

You are my Abba. The more our relationship thrives, the more my pride (deep pleasure in you and your achievements) flourishes. I want to grow in my ability to celebrate who you are and your infinite accomplishments.

Please increase my adoration for you.

I love you,
Mollie

My Child,

I want you to revel in my magnificent presence every day. You were created for so much more than just survival. Don't settle for just going through the motions. You are an eternal creature designed with an eternal capacity to enjoy relationship with me.

When life seems mundane, and you are unfulfilled, it is because you have lost sight of my glory. Ask me to help you refocus on me and the epic adventure we can share. Each day you can enjoy the deep pleasure that comes from sharing life with me and witnessing the mighty works of my hands.

"When life seems mundane, and you are unfulfilled, it is because you have lost sight of my glory."

 I have given you an opportunity to walk alongside me as I free the captives, bind up the brokenhearted, and bring beauty from the ashes of many lives — including yours. Nothing, my child, will satisfy you more than our journey together!

 I love you,
Abba

BRAVE ENOUGH

Where do I find peace and courage?

COURAGE TO SPEAK

"There was a lot of discussion about him among the crowds. Some said, 'He's a wonderful man,' while others said, 'No, he's duping the public.' But no one had the courage to speak out for him in public for fear of reprisals from the Jewish leaders." JOHN 7:12

My Abba,

I realize I am timid to speak of you in situations where I feel like I might face hostility, resistance or ridicule. Usually, there is no substantive threat. Even when people are just disinterested in you, I am prone to keep my mouth shut. The stakes are not high. I am only risking their respect and approval. As I write this, sorrow and embarrassment take turns playing hopscotch in my heart.

I believe I would put everything on the line for you. But my need for approval is obviously getting in the way of sharing your love in these everyday scenarios where your popularity is waning. Sometimes I think I am also concerned about your approval ratings. I don't want to present you in a poor light ... as if you need a campaign manager.

I am constantly sharing my relationship with you in openly receptive situations. But when it comes to some other less friendly contexts, I don't seem to talk about you openly. Please forgive me.

I don't think I have used my opportunities well with people who don't know you. I even change around some family members — not sharing what I think they won't embrace. Please give me your power to shed the chameleon routine.

Show me when to speak and when to remain silent. I want to be sensitive to you, your heart, and how you're leading me. I want others to know and enjoy you as I do, especially the ones who seem to have

no desire to. Remind me when I am reluctant; I was once anything but eager to hear about you.

I love you,
Mollie

My Child,

I desire for you to be strong and very courageous by the power of my Spirit. Don't fear other humans. I am your God. They are not. Don't try to please them.

Public opinion is as fickle as your Texas weather — a silky, gentle breeze one minute, scorching sun the next, followed by a torrential downpour — all before lunch. Managing my image is not your job.

"I love you with an unwavering determination that cannot be tamed."

I am pleased with you. My pleasure in you does not come from your accomplishments. I take pleasure in you because you are mine. You belong to me. I love you with an unwavering determination that cannot be tamed.

That is what I want you to convey to others. Don't worry about damaging my reputation. I have survived thousands of years of atrocities committed on earth in my name. My reputation will not be destroyed by your lack of finesse in presenting the most persuasive, compelling message. Depend on me. It is my job, not yours, to open hearts and minds to my truth.

I just want you to faithfully tell our story. I will give you words to express how much we love each other. As people truly see me and the endless life of joy, grace, love, and peace I offer, many will be drawn to me.

I love you,
Abba

WAITING WELL

"'I will certainly bless you, and I will multiply your descendants beyond number.' Then Abraham waited patiently, and he received what God had promised."
HEBREWS 6:14–15

My Abba,

This verse intrigues me. From my limited vantage point, it doesn't seem like Abraham accepted delays without becoming annoyed or anxious. While he waited on you to supernaturally provide his first descendant, there was the whole "rush to conceive" thing with Hagar. Maybe, Abraham mistook your timing as a divine need for some human intervention. That's convicting.

Thank you for your patience with my impatience. How appropriate that the root of the word patience is "pati," meaning to suffer. For me, waiting patiently can be painful.

I have been thinking this morning about the world in which I live. It is a culture of fast food, high-speed Internet, instant gratification, express service, and overnight delivery. I am trained to believe the majority of things I want can be had almost immediately. I forget my culture can create a ravenous appetite for getting what we want NOW served on a silver platter without much, if any, sacrifice.

Just push a button. Make a call. Click a mouse. Get an App.

But then my culture collides with my personal reality. Unless you intervene, there is no overnight delivery from a neurodegenerative disease. Each day my wait seems to get more arduous and painful. While I look forward to the day you bring me home and gift me with a new

---

WAIT: stay where one is or delay action until a particular time or until something else happens, remain in readiness for some purpose
PATIENT: able to accept or tolerate delays, problems, or suffering without becoming annoyed or anxious, from the Latin word pati: to suffer

body, I desperately need you to hold me up now. I am keenly aware I cannot wait here without you.

    I want to appreciate waiting with you. Please make me more aware of your presence as I struggle with the ache of the wait. When I enjoy your presence, I am able to be content with you, despite the throbbing realities of the present.

    Please give me your contagious joy as we wait together.

I love you,
Mollie

My Child,

Remember, I am not time bound. I don't feel the wait like you do. But I can soothe your soul in your ache of waiting. Don't watch the clock. Focus on my beauty, grace, truth and love. You don't have to wait alone.

> *"I can soothe your soul in your ache of waiting."*

    Patience is a supernatural fruit of my Spirit. Don't try to lasso it in your own strength. You will find that elusive. Walk in my Spirit, looking to me for patience. Then you will be ready for my purposes. If you tie yourself into an anxious knot, you may be distracted and miss our next adventure together.

You know how time flies in the presence of people who delight you. I am perfectly delightful. I can captivate you in a way that will silence the clock. No matter where you are. No matter what you are waiting for (even your new body). No matter how long you wait. I will not abandon you to the struggle. I want you to wait well with me. Let's enjoy the journey together, not just the destination.

I love you,
Abba

BRAVE ENOUGH

"I completely expect and hope that I won't be ashamed in any way. I'm sure I will be brave enough. Now as always Christ will receive glory because of what happens to me. He will receive glory whether I live or die. For me, life finds all of its meaning in Christ. Death also has its benefits." 29 "Here is what he has given you to do for Christ. You must not only believe in him. You must also suffer for him." PHILIPPIANS 1:20–21, 29

My Abba,

I love that the kitten in this photo seems so calm and fearless. It's like he realizes his king-of-the-jungle protection detail is formidable, large and in-charge. At least, that is how the story goes in my imagination.

I know some fear in the right contexts can be healthy. It gives me the sense not to drive into the tornado, play with rattlesnakes, or invite a vicious bully in for tea who's intent on my demise. I like this definition of brave: enduring or facing unpleasant conditions or behavior without being overwhelmed by fear. When I recognize that something is dangerous, or likely to cause pain, but am not debilitated by my emotions, then I think I am moving toward bravery.

I am not a masochist. Physical and emotional pain are definitely not my thing. When pain is mauling my heart, body and/or mind, I need a deeper sense of your gracious presence or I can slip into the vortex of anxiety. I want to be courageous enough to walk faithfully with you, even when my situation is bleak.

I want you to "be lifted high" through my body, whether in health, sickness, or death. I want you to be exalted in my life and

---

BRAVE: enduring or facing unpleasant conditions or behavior without being overwhelmed by fear   FEAR: an unpleasant emotion caused by the belief that someone or something is dangerous, likely to cause pain, or a threat

my death. Please give me the grace to make this a day-to-day reality. Only by your power is this possible.

Let my deepening dependence on you create a valiant heart in me.

I love you,
Mollie

My Child,

Remember, my Son pleaded with me to take the cup of suffering from him. He did not relish the humiliation, pain, and abuse. But he accepted it, because he wanted my will to be done. I did not force him to suffer and die. He chose to walk with me down that road.

Because you have lived with abuse, chronic illness, and tremendous loss, I know you understand suffering. But most of the time, you had no choice. What if, like Christ, you had a choice to take a pass on the painful path to which I called you? What do you think you would do?

Your heart is squirming now, because you realize I know the answer and you are not certain. I understand. Here's reality. If you find your meaning in life through Christ, you will be able to walk with courage through the worst of times, whether you have a choice to be there or not.

You will not be overwhelmed by fear, when your desire to glorify me overwhelms your fear.

By my power, you can live courageously for my plans and purposes. And when your body dies, we can enjoy each other face-to-face forever. All of this struggle will soon vanish. Cling to me. I will hold you. In my arms, you are exceedingly brave!

I love you,
Abba

SOOTHING MY SOUL

"I have told you all this so that you may have peace in me. Here on earth you will have many trials and sorrows. But take heart, because I have overcome the world."
JOHN 16:33

My Child,

I have the power to supernaturally soothe your soul. That is not something the world can offer you. What it has to offer is fleeting and riddled with false promises. Here today and gone tomorrow.

My peace does not vanish when the winds of this world transform the placid lake of your life into anxious waters teeming with whitecaps of many trials and sorrows. Take heart. The peace you find in me gives you rest in the midst of turmoil or tranquility.

> *"The peace you find in me gives you rest in the midst of turmoil or tranquility."*

I have overcome all of the darkness this world has to offer and can give you peace that is not dependent on cashmere conditions. As you grow more and more determined to live for my glory, you will be caught up in my supernatural, invincible peace. And that peace will carry you through the most challenging of life's gauntlets.

I love you,
Abba

PEACE: freedom from disturbance, a state of being at rest

My Abba,

I want what you have to offer me. When I look at the definitions of peace, I think "freedom from disturbance" sounds nice. But what I want even more than that is a "state of being at rest." I want to be at rest in you even when there is not freedom from disturbance.

When I am truly at rest, I am restored and renewed.

I don't want to live without your supernatural soothing of my soul. I need your comfort and rest when life is uncomfortable. But I want it all the time — whether life feels like I am crawling across steel wool or satin sheets. I want all situations to point me to you. I want to sense your love, provision, pleasure, and peace amidst all my experiences. I don't want to waste precious moments without you.

I am reminded of a prayer I wrote a few years back. It is the cry of my heart again today:

God, I am here to glorify you, not me. Show me how my circumstances would look different to me, if glorifying you were my highest priority. When my life is heavy with pain, please make my question, "How," not "Why?" "How can I glorify you in the midst of this trial?" Instead of, "Why is this happening?" Please give me the supernatural peace of your Holy Spirit in exchange for my pain. Wash away what is not of you. Cleanse my heart. Make me new.

I love anticipating what will be up ahead on this journey with you. No matter what the next bend in the road brings, you will be there and it will be permeated with your glory.

Thank you for a peace-filled future.

I love you,
Mollie

SURPRISING SUPERHEROES

"We are human, but we don't wage war as humans do. We use God's mighty weapons, not worldly weapons, to knock down the strongholds of human reasoning and to destroy false arguments."
2 CORINTHIANS 10:3–4

My Child,

Although you live as a human, you cannot effectively wage war in your human strength. Your adversary is not flesh and blood. Fighting someone who has supernatural powers with your natural weapons will lead you to defeat.

I provide you with supernatural weapons (not weapons crafted with human hands) to knock down the strongholds in your life. These are places in your journey that our enemy has fortified, in order, to try to protect them from your attempts to disrupt his plans.

"Only I can truly make you battle ready."

My supernatural weapons look quite different from weapons used for conventional warfare. Our enemy's strategies can only be effective, if you try to fight it out on your own with the wrong weapons.

Only I can truly make you battle ready. I can equip you by the power of my Spirit with a supernatural arsenal. Defenders like truth, righteousness, peace, faith, and perseverance can be part of your

---

STRONGHOLD: a place that has been fortified so as to protect it against attack   SUPERHERO: a benevolent character with superhuman powers

protection. But I can also give you supernatural weapons like love, humility, forgiveness, patience, mercy, kindness, joy, wisdom, faithfulness, compassion and hope. My powerful gifts are invaluable in any situation, but especially when you are in the thick of battle.

Through my power, we can destroy strongholds that impede your relationship with others and me. Take captive your rebellious thoughts and bring them to me. My peace will be yours as you live under my authority.

I am the ultimate expert on how to live life. I created all life and have been perfectly acquainted with human behavior from the beginning. I know how this works.

I have flawless clarity on the difference between right and wrong. I have unsurpassed insight and wisdom. Stay in step with me and you will walk into increasing power and freedom.

I love you,
Abba

My Abba,

I have learned when I march each day onto the battlefield of life I will get pummeled, if I don't rely on you. I accept your truth. I need your supernatural protection and power to do battle with a supernatural enemy. Please make me fit for battle today.

By your power, I ask you to direct and equip me. Enliven my heart to your voice. I want to live in peaceful, power-filled surrender to you, the King of the Universe.

As I think about how my children pretended to be their favorite superheroes, it occurs to me that living life supernaturally sustained by your infinite, endless power gives all your children the opportunity to be superheroes. We can be transformed into "benevolent characters with superhuman powers."

By your power, we can love the unlovely, forgive the unforgivable, bring peace in the chaos, sow justice in the most inhospitable ground, inspire hope in the hopeless, and move that mountain that looks like it won't budge an inch. Especially now in the midst of our heartbreaking landscape, we need you to empower us to make a lasting difference in this world.

Although it sounds marvelous to fly above the fray, hair and cape blowing in the wind, please continue to show me every day the stunning opportunities you give me to live life on the ground, in the heat of the battle, fueled by your matchless power.

I love you,
Mollie

GLIMMER IN THE DARK

How do I keep my eyes on eternity?

OBSESSED WITH MY PRIZE

"So we don't look at the troubles we can see now;
rather, we fix our gaze on things that cannot be seen.
For the things we see now will soon be gone,
but the things we cannot see will last forever."
2 CORINTHIANS 4:18

My Abba,

This verse brings to mind a conversation I had a while back with a friend. "I don't have the awe and wonder you have for God," she said.

That comment brought up several thoughts for me. I was deeply grateful for the gift of sight that you have given me. I notice (in some infantile way) how delightfully perfect you are. I was grateful that something about the way you and I connect convinced her I experience awe and wonder for you. I was grateful for the way her words encouraged me to keep my gaze fixed on you, my eternal God. Not just for my pleasure, but so others might see it is possible to experience that awe and wonder.

"Please fuel my passion for what is unseen, glorious and eternal."

I always want to remember that mug of White Rose tea on the table at Kerbey Lane cafe, as my friend and I spoke. I said, "Let's imagine that I believe this mug is the single most beautiful, pleasurable, valuable treasure in all of the universe. And let's say this mug has the power to transform me into the most glorious version of myself and give me eternal joy.

"What if I realized that there were obstacles between this glorious treasure and me? I would want to recognize those objects and remove them in order to see, enjoy, and be transformed by this priceless treasure. I would be driven to find and remove those obstacles. That would not be a duty I pursued because someone guilted me into it. I would be on a mission — obsessed with my prize."

I don't know if my illustration changed my friend's perspective. But the recalling of it encourages me. Please fuel my passion for what is unseen, glorious and eternal.

I love you,
Mollie

My Child,

You are beginning to notice how much your focus impacts you. It directs, affects, and informs your path. When your gaze is locked on something, or someone, you don't have the mind space to give attention to much else. The more you fix your eyes on me, the more you see what is important to me.

The company you keep influences you. When you choose to enjoy my company, my presence changes you, making you more like me. My beauty draws you in, and helps you release what is false and not of me.

As you enjoy my embrace, those distractions over there in the shadows will look like what they really are — god frauds. They caught your attention when you were tempted to see me as dissatisfying, ineffective, slow, or disinterested.

It doesn't mean I am not paying attention because I don't part the waters when you want me to. When I don't move that mountain, it does not indicate I lack compassion or am somehow inept or shorthanded.

Remember, my thoughts are not your thoughts. My ways are not your ways. Sometimes the pain of this world tries to herd your thoughts into a pen of despair. Even when you don't understand the "whys," I am asking you to trust my character.

Stay close. The more you are with me, the more you will see me for who I am. That wisdom will help you to trust me for what you cannot see.

I love you,
Abba

REAL LIFE

"For you died to this life, and your real life is hidden with Christ in God. And when Christ, who is your life, is revealed to the whole world, you will share in all his glory." COLOSSIANS 3:3–4

My Child,

When Christ is your life, you enjoy freedom from the tyranny of your circumstances. If your heart and mind are set on his glory, then your life becomes a beautiful stage for my show-stopping miracles.

Don't set your heart on what is vulnerable to moths, rust, or thieves. Pour your heart, mind and soul into that which lasts forever. You have died to this life. Live like it.

Transcending your circumstances will come when you fix your gaze on me. I am with you in the hurricane of your pain. What you first perceive as a prison can be a platform for praise.

> *"What you first perceive as a prison can be a platform for praise."*

You have the privilege of experiencing my love, and then showing others how I am working in and through you. You can choose real life — to thrive by the power of my Spirit as a conduit of my love, grace, and truth. Or, you can try to subsist apart from me with your sparse resources.

You have experienced both paths. The choice is yours. Which path will you walk today? I can empower you to choose well. Just ask.

I love you,
Abba

My Abba,

Yes, I have experienced both paths. When I take my eyes off you, the slightest hiccup can throw me into the ditch. It doesn't really take much at all. Without your glorious presence, past pain alone would be enough to snuff out my joy for a lifetime.

Thank you that I don't have to face my past, present or future without you! With you, there is no downside. No dark side. No hidden agenda. No weakness that will come to light under closer inspection.

When I draw near to you, I get to experience the Only One in the universe who is flawless. Why would I ever choose to run from you? The running seems to happen when I entertain the company of two lies. The first is when I believe the lie that something, or someone, who is imperfect is going to meet my needs better than someone who is perfect. Illogical, I know. And the second lie is equally illogical. I somehow believe the lie that I can't, or shouldn't, come to you because I don't meet your standards.

Please lift the smog of this half-truth our enemy attempts to breathe into my mind. I know the whole truth is this: I don't meet your standards. I am imperfect. But you made a perfect way for me to be a part of your forever family through Jesus Christ.

Thank you that beloved children don't have to beg for a spot at their father's table. Thank you that I can bring all the blemished, bruised parts of me and still receive your gracious welcome. Remind me (again and again) that I have a relationship with you because of what you, not I, bring to the table.

I love you,
Mollie

LONGING FOR LIGHT

"Then the angel showed me a river with the water of life, clear as crystal, flowing from the throne of God and of the Lamb. It flowed down the center of the main street. On each side of the river grew a tree of life, bearing twelve crops of fruit, with a fresh crop each month. The leaves were used for medicine to heal the nations.

"No longer will there be a curse upon anything. For the throne of God and of the Lamb will be there, and his servants will worship him. And they will see his face, and his name will be written on their foreheads. And there will be no night there — no need for lamps or sun — for the Lord God will shine on them. And they will reign forever and ever." REVELATION 22:1-5

My Abba,

I rejoice that you are the God of my forever. I love that you are not just here today and gone tomorrow. You are beyond awesome, and you will never abandon me. Your faithfulness is impressive to me — especially when a betrayal hits close to home.

Reading about heaven today gives me renewed stamina to run this race. I love those you have placed in my life, but I have to admit I want to be free of this world's struggle and pain. I long for the river of life — clear as crystal, flowing from your throne. I long for a healed body, free from disease.

What will it be like to be free from the curse of sin and death? I truly can't imagine. But the idea of nothing impeding communion with you sounds magnificent.

    I can't wait for the day when my identity will be completely immersed in yours. I love the image of your name written on my forehead — your everlasting autograph demonstrating to all of creation, for all time, that I belong to you. Thank you that there will be a time when your light will banish all our confusion and darkness, and we will live fully in the radiance of your presence.

    Today may be a struggle, but the truth about my forever spurs me on. By the power of your Spirit, I can wait and walk this arduous path with you until I get to the other side. Please while I am here, though, let me enter into the joy of glorifying you, whether that is in trial, tragedy or triumph.

    I love you,
    Mollie

My Child,

I am sorry you have endured the bitter sting of betrayal. I know how painful that can be. Remember not to dress me in their garments. I am not a betrayer. I will not break my promises or turn my back on you. That is not who I am.

    You can trust me when I say we will spend a spectacular eternity together. I know, at times, your circumstances can feel grueling. But that pain will evaporate like a drop of water in the blaze of a fierce summer sun at the first taste of eternity.

Nothing on earth can give you an accurate picture of what heaven will be like. Seeing me face to face will change everything. No bleak chasms will scar the landscape of your life. My light will dispel them all.

> *"No bleak chasms will scar the landscape of your life. My light will dispel them all."*

The glorious things you would like to be and do will no longer be illusive. No striving, suffering or sadness. Just unhindered joy, love and peace. Christ has made a way for you to fully enjoy me and all my gifts — forever.

That is your future. And it will be worth the wait.

I love you,

Abba

CAPTIVE GAZE

"Think about the things of heaven,
not the things of earth." COLOSSIANS 3:2

My Abba,

When I look back on what I have allowed to dominate my mind over the years, I know I have not always invested myself well. Many times, I have *not* set my affections — my heart and mind — on what is precious to you. I have not focused on who you are and what you desire.

But when I truly embrace reality, you are the only one with whom I continually want to fill my mind. Then all this perishing window dressing moves into proper perspective. Please don't let me obsess about earthly things. I don't want to belong to, be held captive by, or be dominated by them.

> *"Don't let me be tempted by a timeshare in a fool's paradise. Anchor me in the reality of your love."*

I confess that sometimes I wake up and am beguiled by the samba of the mundane. When I am not looking for you, I can wind up dancing with the dust bunnies of life. Not my best choice of partners.

Other times, I am dominated by the throb of pain and disappointment. I can't seem to look away. Then there are the times when I find myself zeroing-in on your good gifts, to the exclusion of you, the generous Giver. I know when that happens, I have missed the foremost point of your generosity.

I don't want to go back to ignoring, denying, and pretending that life with all its pain and promise is not happening. I just want to give

my heart and mind to you and not to the battering ram of my circumstances. Please rescue me today from the foolish idols that besiege me.

Don't let me be tempted by a timeshare in a fool's paradise. Anchor me in the reality of your love.

I love you,
Mollie

My Child,

You know from your dance training that you will move toward the object on which you "spot" or focus, when doing turns across the floor. You stare at one spot as long as you can when turning, and then snap your head back around to refocus on that spot. If you practice that relentlessly, you succeed in moving gracefully across the floor.

But remember how dizzy you became when you lost your "spot"? You would either wind up sprawled out on the floor or, if you managed to stay on your feet, clutching the wall while trying not to reveal to others that your world was spinning out of control.

The music of this world taps out a fast, delirious rhythm. You will lose your balance, if you set your eyes on the scenery or circumstances around you. When subtle distractors or strong-armed captors surround and harass you, don't lose your focus. Set your sights on me. I am the only one worthy of your captive gaze.

I love you,
Abba

RELAXING CLENCHED FISTS

"The man replied, 'I've obeyed all these commandments since I was young.' When Jesus heard his answer, he said, 'There is still one thing you haven't done. Sell all your possessions and give the money to the poor, and you will have treasure in heaven. Then come, follow me.' But when the man heard this he became very sad, for he was very rich." LUKE 18:21–23

My Abba,

As I meditated on this passage, I wondered what would be considered "very rich" in our world today? The answer I found makes me recognize how numb I am to the wealth I wade in. It appears that an average median household income worldwide is about $10,000. Although the statistics I found are a few years old, they are still convicting.

In light of this sobering reality, I started noticing the extravagant ways I live as a "very rich" woman. I used running water this morning — hot and cold. I have indoor plumbing with a functional toilet, shower, and dishwasher. I didn't have to build a fire to cook my breakfast this morning. I had access to healthy food I took out of a refrigerator, which kept it from spoiling overnight. Rain does not leak through my roof. The temperature inside my home is pleasant because I have a heating and cooling system. My washing machine is laboring for me while I type on my computer.

So how is it that I still wrestle at times to surrender discontentment to you? That embarrasses me. I want to think I am too spiritual to struggle with materialism. I want to believe I am clearly more committed to treasure in heaven than on earth. But how would I feel if you

asked me to sell everything and give the profit away? Like the man in this passage, would I be distraught because I believe my possessions make me happy?

> *"So how is it that I still wrestle at times to surrender discontentment to you?"*

I have to admit I am wiggling a bit under the weight of these questions. Please give me a grateful heart for all your provision today. Spiritually. Emotionally. Physically. I want my heart to be content — like yours.

I love you,
Mollie

My Child,

The first step to having the freedom to lay down what you desire is to actually recognize what you desire. You cannot experience my contentment by pretending or burying desire.

It has taken you some time (and healing) to get here. You can't relinquish the wants you don't know you have. Realizing your desire is a healthy step.

I want you to acknowledge your desire and then honestly release it to me. If it is eternally useful, I can keep it in your life. If not, why would you want to hang on to something that will fill your tiny hands with what is perishable and fleeting?

I did not create you to clutch earthly things. Clenched fists will leave you with cramped hands. And many times, you will destroy what you seize in your hungry grip. What you envision as the perfect possessions will never give you the joy you can experience participating with me in my plans and purposes.

Keep your hands relaxed and wide open. I will fill them with unimaginable treasure that will never fade or fail.

I love you,
Abba

NEON LIGHTS

"Do not love this world nor the things it offers you, for when you love the world, you do not have the love of the Father in you. For the world offers only a craving for physical pleasure, a craving for everything we see, and pride in our achievements and possessions. These are not from the Father, but are from this world. And this world is passing away, along with everything that people crave."
1 JOHN 2:15–17a

My Child,

I have blessed you with limitless gifts. From dawn's dewdrops sprinkled like diamonds across green blades of nascent grass to colossal mountain ranges marching victoriously into a blazing sunset. From the delight of the first smile on a new baby's lips to the twilight happiness of a life well lived.

I want you to enjoy (take pleasure) in these gifts from me. But I don't want you to give yourself to the gifts. Out of my love for you, I bless you with relationships, experiences and pleasures. My desire is that those blessings will fan the flame of adoration and worship of me.

This world offers you many opportunities to devote yourself to created things. Don't be deceived. Fleeting experiences, achievements or possessions cannot satisfy that craving in your belly. Pinning all your hopes on drifting pleasures will leave you brokenhearted. How brittle these people, places, and things are when the weight of all your desire and expectation bears down on them. That pressure causes things to fracture and fade.

LOVE: *devotion, adoration, worship; liking, enjoyment, taking pleasure in*

Your desires are not too grand. But at times you may look to satisfy them in the wrong places. You were made to crave the magnificent, endless waterfall of my presence. You can't find that in the mouth of a dripping faucet.

I love you,
Abba

My Abba,

I appreciate the clarity you brought me this morning on the different ways we use the word "love." I want to crave and worship only you. But transient treasures capture my eyes at times with their glittering promises of fulfillment. They hype a quick road to contentment.

Sometimes I feel like I am walking through a carnival. Brightly painted, flashing facades, cotton candy, spinning rides, smoke and mirrors. Perhaps fun for a moment, but do I really desire to live on a ferris wheel?

In my heart of hearts, I want what will still be illuminated by your love when the neon of this world sputters out. Show me how to invest in what is true and eternally tangible. Fading accomplishments on this temporal timeline will never satisfy my eternal longings. I am a forever creature made for forever purposes.

Point me to the endless views of your kingdom. Give me your eyes to see and your ears to hear today. By your Spirit, please unveil an enduring radiance in me that invites others to enjoy your glorious, inexplicable light.

I love you,
Mollie

GLIMMER IN THE DARK

"That is why they stand in front of God's throne and serve him day and night in his Temple. And he who sits on the throne will give them shelter. They will never again be hungry or thirsty; they will never be scorched by the heat of the sun. For the Lamb on the throne will be their Shepherd. He will lead them to springs of life-giving water. And God will wipe every tear from their eyes."
REVELATION 7: 15–17

My Abba,

This portrait of heaven overwhelms me. When I get the slightest glimpse of what it might be like to live with you in heaven, it is almost too much for me to bear. I cannot speak. I weep with joy. I feel like my fragile frame may come undone.

More and more, I understand why this is my experience. You are perfectly beautiful in every way. That is who you are. So, being overwhelmed by a glimpse of such magnificence is understandable.

I hear some, who report to believe in you, say, "Growing old is better than the alternative!" That shows our incredible lack of understanding about heaven. It breaks my heart.

Immerse our hearts in the unspeakable joy of your presence so that we may understand, in some small way, the fullness of joy that will be possible when we see you face to face. Please help this homesick child to be on a wondrous journey with you today exploring your beauty and entering into the joy of glorifying you.

Write your name all over my day.

I love you,
Mollie

My Child,

You can't imagine the experience of heaven. It is beyond your most untamed, spectacular dreams. Heaven is not just an absence of tears, hunger, thirst, the scorching sun of suffering, and all evil. It is the perfect symphony of love, grace, joy, beauty, justice, mercy, and peace — uninterrupted, always.

I want the reality of heaven to nourish your heart when things are rough. But I also want you to enjoy my presence now, even in the midst of pain that may feel like a battering ram on the front door of your heart. You don't have to wait until you see me face to face to experience the joy of knowing me.

> "One day, you will stand before my throne eternally sheltered and utterly free."

On days where you feel bound to what appears to be a less than ideal life, look to me, the Author of Life. Even on this side of heaven, I can infuse life into places where death seems to circle you.

Nothing that wars against you can stand against me. I have no worthy opponents. Come to me with the tamest of skirmishes and the brutal, full-scale wars.

One day, you will stand before my throne eternally sheltered and utterly free. But until then, remember we are still inseparable. And together, we can do this.

I love you,
Abba

LIFE SUPPORT

How do I depend on God?

STRONG MEDICINE

"Praise be to the God and Father of our Lord Jesus Christ, the Father of compassion and the God of all comfort, who comforts us in all our troubles, so that we can comfort those in any trouble with the comfort we ourselves have received from God. For just as we share abundantly in the sufferings of Christ, so also our comfort abounds through Christ."
2 CORINTHIANS 1:3–5

My Abba,

I praise you this morning for you are my God. Everything good in my life arises from your compassionate hands. I know well what it is like to be carried by your comfort.

You have crawled with me through some thorn-filled gauntlets in my life. You have rescued me from indescribable pain, drawn out poison, and bandaged my wounds. You are my strong medicine! The one who mends my ailing heart and mind.

The trouble in this world does not take a time out, recess, or holiday. But fortunately, you don't either. Thank you that you have compassion for me. You suffer with me when I suffer. Thank you that you are always there to ease my pain, to offer me your joy, and to strengthen me.

I love the fact that the root of the word for comfort is "fortis" meaning strong. You make me stronger as you soothe my pain. And from that place, you give me the opportunity to partner with you in soothing the wounds of others. Thank you for allowing me to pass on

---

COMPASSION: sorrow and concern for the sufferings or misfortunes of others Origin: Latin compassio(n-), from compati 'suffer with.'
COMFORT: to make someone feel less unhappy, help someone feel more at ease, from late Latin confortare: strengthen, From com- (expressing intensive force) + Latin fortis: strong.

your comfort and strength to others who feel crushed by the weight of this world.

Please be the healing balm that flows through me to those who are hurting.

I love you,
Mollie

My Child,

I always stand ready to be a wellspring of comfort to you. I know sometimes you feel battered by adversaries as you make your way through this life. Your battle is real. But some things that appear to be allies are not.

Don't look to them for comfort. Their anesthesia might make you feel less pain for a moment, but that power quickly fades. Mine does not. My comfort is endless and eternal.

> *"I always stand ready to be a wellspring of comfort to you."*

Keep looking to me. I provide a remedy that actually grows more potent over time. Then you can be a conduit of my comfort to others.

I will still be the source. But you will have the opportunity to allow my grace to flow through you. I will give you my compassion, so you have supernatural mercy to share with those in pain.

I don't want you to be crushed as you care for those I place in your life. Let me hoist your back-breaking burdens onto my shoulders. I will never be weighed down. No burden is more than I can bear.

I love you,
Abba

BETTER THAN LIFE

"You, God, are my God, earnestly I seek you; I thirst for you, my whole being longs for you, in a dry and parched land where there is no water. I have seen you in the sanctuary and beheld your power and your glory. Because your love is better than life, my lips will glorify you. I will praise you as long as I live, and in your name I will lift up my hands. I will be fully satisfied as with the richest of foods; with singing lips my mouth will praise you. On my bed I remember you; I think of you through the watches of the night. Because you are my help, I sing in the shadow of your wings. I cling to you; your right hand upholds me" PSALM 63:1-8

My Abba,

It feels odd to respond to this psalm on the page. Thank you for waking me every morning for so many years with this life-giving prayer on my lips. It is definitely the most transformative passage I have ever memorized. Even after all these years though, I know you can give me an eager heart, open to your truth. Please provide a fresh perspective.

I love how it begins. "You, God, are my God." You are not some comic-book deity we conjured up to entertain us with a few flashy superpowers. You are the one true perfect, infinite, eternal God who spoke the constellations into being. And you are my God! The Limitless One who sings over the universe and holds all things together, also makes melody in this one finite, human heart. I am yours and you are mine. Loving Creator and beloved created one inseparable forever! This truth leaves me awestruck and delighted.

Thank you that most days I experience an earnest desire to connect with you. But when I don't, please carry my true longing into the light. Even when I can't recognize what my heart truly craves amidst the crooked commotion of life, I know my desire for you doesn't disappear.

Whether I recognize it or not, you are always the one for whom I hunger and thirst. You satisfy my soul.

It's just that sometimes I allow our enemy (that street-slick scam artist) to sell me a dreadful knockoff that promises to please. When that happens, I miss the real deal. Open the eyes of my heart. Without you, I will settle for forged goods.

It was always easy for me to believe a love relationship with you was better than the black and blue, bruised-up chapters of my journey. But thank you for ultimately showing me your perfect love is better than, even the most "ideal" life I could dream up.

I can honestly say now, I would not trade your flawless love for a flawless life.

I love you,
Mollie

My Child,

You used to withhold parts of your heart because you believed there were people, achievements, and possessions you would find more appealing than me. I was your back-up plan when the world broke your heart. You wanted me to wait quietly in the wings so you could signal me for the rescue when the villains were overtaking you. But the hero is not a nameless extra in your supporting cast.

I take joy in your change of heart. Now that you savor the taste of my presence, you spend more time with me and are increasingly aware of who I am. You can celebrate me forever. My perfection never runs dry.

Always remember the way your babies would cling to you as you carried them. They instinctively knew to do that. That is how I want you to cling to me. I will continue to cultivate that instinct in you. But just as they did not have the strength to hold on without help, you don't either. Cling to me. I will uphold you with my mighty right hand.

I love you,
Abba

LIFE SUPPORT

"He remembered us in our weakness.
His faithful love endures forever.
He saved us from our enemies.
His faithful love endures forever." PSALM 136:23-24

My Abba,

My heart and mind are sputtering this morning. I find myself utterly weak and disoriented after trying to navigate a few hours under my own steam. Yesterday, I chose you and your resources, and my day was brimming with peace.

This morning I kept thinking, "I just need to tend to this one more thing and then I can give you my full attention." One "urgent" task led to another, one phone call to another, and one emergency to another. Yesterday I handled those things while enjoying your presence — consistently going to you for the next step and solution. I was smiling at day's end.

Today I waver between wanting to hunker down under the covers or make my great escape to some fantastical, trouble-free paradise. My enemies — the daily irritants, middleweight dilemmas, and high-octane heartbreakers create a voracious herd. I am no match. My spirit, mind, and body feel like I need life support. I guess I should hold that thought. You are definitely my life support.

You always remember my utter weakness, but sometimes I forget. This morning I am, once again, acutely aware of my desperate dependence. Utter weakness calls for utter dependency. Am I overwhelmed more easily than others? Or, am I just addicted (bound) to your presence? Perhaps, it is both.

I have tasted and seen I cannot thrive without your living water. My sensitivity may make it more difficult to do life without you. I find this journey excruciating at times. It seems "do or die" with me. I do relationship with you, or die to any semblance of an abundant life.

So today I choose life. I choose the joy of losing myself in your love. I know this glorious experience will cause me to crave you tomorrow, even more than today. I rejoice that there is no limit to the pleasure of your presence!

I love you,
Mollie

My Child,

I am glad you want to be with me. I want you to enjoy our relationship as much as I do. The hills and valleys of your day will become less impediment, and more adventure, as we walk them together.

If you allow my Spirit to guide you, you won't see trials as menacing enemies poised to rob you of your joy. Think of these troubles (small and immense) as opportunities to create, cooperate, and participate with me. My faithful love endures forever.

There will be no shortage of tomorrow's trials. But the more you immerse yourself in the refreshing waters of my love, the more you will find rest in me.

Think of when you traveled to the Caribbean — a powder blue sky, dazzling sunlight, and warm ivory beaches embraced by aquamarine waves. You found it exciting and restful — all at the same time. That is how life can be with me. I can inspire your soul to sing amidst the tumult of churning tides or the stillness of glassy seas.

I love you,
Abba

BE MY RESCUE

"For you have rescued me from death;
you have kept my feet from slipping.
So now I can walk in your presence, O God,
in your life-giving light." PSALM 56:13

My Abba,

I am immeasurably grateful that your once-and-for-all rescue through Christ brought me into a forever, life-giving relationship with you. Thank you for rescuing me from eternal death.

The endless absence of your presence is not something I would want for my worst enemy. I cannot conceive of an eternal void of love, joy, beauty, pleasure, peace, kindness, goodness, and faithfulness — everything you are.

> *"Your vibrant Spirit animates my heart and mind with the joy of true freedom."*

But I realize your rescue is also a daily rhythm. Each day you give me the opportunity to choose what brings life or what does not.

So many lifeless beauties hiding behind perfectly painted masks vie for my attention. They strut through my life every day howling about their ability to satisfy my soul. You never howl at me. You just offer to quietly escort me into life. Your vibrant Spirit animates my heart and mind with the joy of true freedom.

When I walk in your presence, I always find your life-giving light to be perfectly authentic. No false advertising. You are end-

---

RESCUE: save someone from a dangerous or distressing situation, keep from being lost or abandoned   TRUST: a firm belief in the strength, truth, ability, or reliability of someone or something

lessly better than the best opinion I could ever form of you. Please liberate me from all the ways I settle for what is less than you and your desires for me. Keep my feet from slipping. Captivate my heart. Be my Rescue.

I love you,
Mollie

My Child,

You don't have to wait until you are free from your journey on earth to enjoy the life I offer. Our relationship is forever and now.

I want to be on adventure with you every day rescuing you from the imitations and counterfeits — the man-made life for which you might be tempted to settle. Sometimes when you are in a dangerous or distressing situation, you don't realize it. My rescue can appear misguided, confusing or disappointing to you. I want you to remember I am always trustworthy even when you can't make sense of things. I am infinitely strong, truthful, able and reliable.

One way you might try to cope with the pain of your today is to live in tomorrow. But that strategy robs you of the joy I have for you in the present. If your eyes are always fixed on the future, you will miss the beauty you can experience with me today. Even when the trail is rough, there is splendor in my presence.

I can show you my magnificence as we traverse smooth meadows or saw-toothed cliffs. Let me reveal what you cannot see with human eyes. Walk with me today in my life-giving light. I am your Rescue.

I love you,
Abba

PROMISE KEEPER

"Don't put your confidence in powerful people;
there is no help for you there. When they breathe their last,
they return to the earth, and all their plans die with them.
But joyful are those who have the God of Israel as their helper,
whose hope is in the Lord their God. He made heaven
and earth, the sea, and everything in them.
He keeps every promise forever."
PSALM 146:3–6

My Child,

At times your head is turned by the power of man. I know from your perspective people can look very impressive. Man may inflict great pain or bring significant reward. But remember the most powerful human is still flesh and blood and dependent on me for their next breath.

People come and go. But I am.

Unlike people, I will never perish, diminish, or change. Many times, humans commit to do a particular thing or guarantee something will happen. But in reality, they don't have that kind of power. They can have the best intentions and promise to try, but something may thwart their success.

Nothing thwarts me. I have always been and will always be God. I will accomplish what I set out to do. I want to draw you into my forever plans today. I promise you my endless grace, truth and love. And I don't just make promises. I keep them. Because of who I am, I cannot slip up, falter, or betray you.

PROMISE: a declaration or assurance that one will do a particular thing or that a particular thing will happen

Put your hope in me — the one who has the power to hold the galaxies in place. I promise I can handle the challenges of your day, no matter what comes along.

I love you,
Abba

My Abba,

I realize I can get caught up in the power of man, at times. There are even powerful people in my family in whom I am tempted to put my confidence. I know you can use them to accomplish great things. But please help me to see all humans as part of my earth troop and reserve the God space only for you.

I need your intervention today, my all powerful, promise-keeping God. I feel frail and keenly aware of my humanity. I cannot run this race without you. Please take me and what you want me to accomplish today and fuel it by your power and love.

I really do believe you are my only hope. I just get distracted from that truth, sometimes. You have the integrity and power to make promises and keep them.

So today, I don't want to put my confidence in what I perceive as the best and most powerful tools, systems, conveniences and circumstances created by man. Give me the wisdom not to trust in dust. I want to put my hope in you, my God, who made humans, earth, sea, space, and everything else.

Thank you that you will never leave me or forsake me. No shift in my universe will alter who you are — Never-Changing, Always-Faithful God. Please give me everything I need to put my confidence in you.

I love you,
Mollie

MY REMEDY

"When Jesus heard this, he told them, 'Healthy people don't need a doctor — sick people do. I have come to call not those who think they are righteous, but those who know they are sinners.'" MARK 2:17

My Child,

I rejoiced with the angels the day you embraced the truth of your condition. I reached out. You took my hand. You understood your soul was too sick for a human remedy. You accepted the reality that you missed the mark of my perfection and needed a supernatural intervention. When you surrendered to my care, I flooded your heart with the eternal cure for your sin sickness.

I am also your daily remedy, no matter what plagues you. Your ultimate spiritual, emotional and physical healing will take place when we see each other face to face. But even now, you can experience the stunning ways I can cause you to thrive as you pursue my glory.

> *"I flooded your heart with the eternal cure for your sin sickness."*

Our enemy still seeks to infect you with his malicious viruses of hate, despair, anxiety, jealousy and pride. But as you are increasingly dependent on me, I will boost your spiritual immune system.

The attacks will continue, but you will enjoy greater vigor as you sip from the pure, healing water of my presence. Come to me and drink.

I love you,
Abba

REMEDY: a medicine or treatment for a disease or injury, a means of counteracting or eliminating something undesirable, to set right

My Abba,

Maybe the reason this analogy remains powerful for me is because I have struggled with chronic illness for so many years. I am keenly aware of what it's like to be sick. And, since I live with diseases doctors don't know how to cure, I am not accustomed to depending on humans for healing. You are my only viable physical, emotional and spiritual remedy.

As I think about it, though, I wasn't just spiritually sick when you rescued me. It was worse than that. I was past the point of recovery. I was actually dead in my sin. Since dead people can't do anything for themselves, I certainly could not make myself come alive. I needed a whole new life. When it comes to resurrection, you are the only competent one. Thank you for doing for me what I could never do for myself.

Please help me to see my day-to-day desperate dependence on you as the gift that it is. Then I will not despise the path of suffering that brought me to this divine place where I am utterly reliant on you. Please anoint my heart with the soothing oil of your presence. Cause your love to saturate the injured places in my heart, mind and body, to comfort and bring new life.

And when denial rears its cunning head and I don't see the dire straits I am in, please disturb my delusion. Revive me. Wake me to the wonder of you.

I love you,
Mollie

INSEPARABLE

"What shall we say about such wonderful things as these? If God is for us, who can ever be against us?"

"Can anything ever separate us from Christ's love? Does it mean he no longer loves us if we have trouble or calamity, or are persecuted, or hungry, or destitute, or in danger, or threatened with death?"

"And I am convinced that nothing can ever separate us from God's love. Neither death nor life, neither angels nor demons, neither our fears for today nor our worries about tomorrow—not even the powers of hell can separate us from God's love. No power in the sky above or in the earth below—indeed, nothing in all creation will ever be able to separate us from the love of God that is revealed in Christ Jesus our Lord."
ROMANS 8:31, 35, 38–39

My Child,

I am for you, not against you. I want to remind you of some of the "wonderful things" with which I bless you as my child.

- The gift of my Spirit as a foretaste of future glory
- No condemnation
- Glorious freedom from the power of sin, death and decay
- Power to walk in my Spirit and please me
- My Spirit pleading for you in harmony with my will
- No obligation to obey your sinful nature

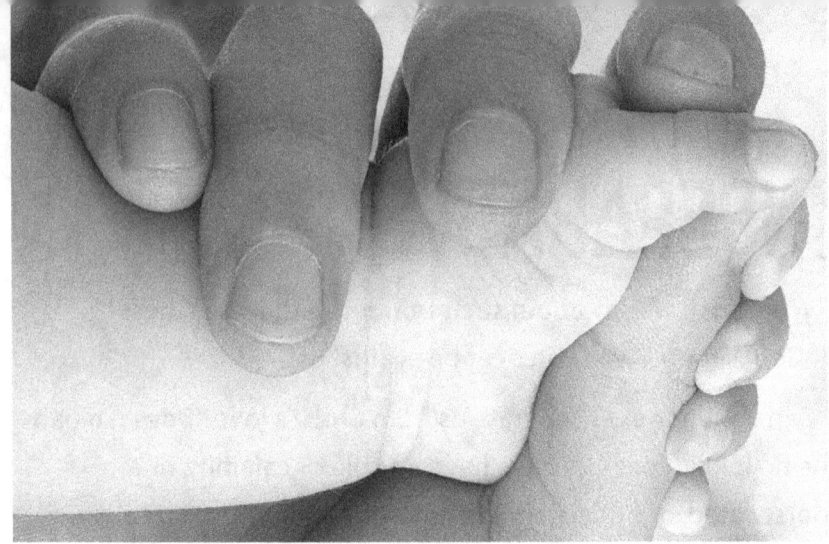

- Affirmation that you are mine
- Eager hope for your full rights as an adopted child and joint heir
- Eternity in my presence

These are just a few of my gifts spawned by my endless, flawless love for you. The most formidable obstacles in the universe will never keep us apart.

When you accepted my invitation, I made my home in you. We are now inseparable. What I have joined together, nothing, no one, can divide.

When you take the wrong path, you feel estranged from me. But I will never leave you or forsake you. It's like when your poor choices make you feel separated from a loved one who is sitting in the same room with you. Their presence does not make you feel close. You feel miles apart, even though you are still family.

That is how it is for us. Sometimes your misdeeds impede our intimacy, but we are inextricably connected. Lay that thing down. It will never satisfy you.

I am right here. In my presence there is pleasure forever.

I love you,

Abba

My Abba,

All accusations, adversaries, rejection, and confrontation pales in comparison to your advocacy. Thank you that distressing circumstances do not indicate a lapse in your love for me. Thank you that when life gets difficult, it isn't because you forgot to pay attention. Thank you that when adversity comes, it does not mean you are averse to me.

Thank you that when I have trouble, it doesn't mean I am in trouble with you. Thank you that when I feel rejected, I am still your honored child. Thank you that when all seems threatened, you are never concerned your plans will be thwarted in my life. Somehow you will accomplish all that you desire in, and through, me.

I know you live in me but sometimes I can feel distant from you. Experientially, I can feel detached. I do believe no power that exists can separate us. But at times, my sin can get in the way, creating static in our connection. Clearly, not a good choice for me.

I want to enjoy vibrant communion with you today. Please continually infuse me with a supernatural awareness of the joy that is mine through an intimate relationship with you. Each day, I want to increasingly savor and celebrate that reality.

I love you,
Mollie

SHIFTING SHADOWS & HEAVENLY LIGHTS

What happens when I get it wrong?

FOOLING OURSELVES

"Suppose we claim we are without sin. Then we are fooling ourselves. The truth is not in us. But God is faithful and fair. If we confess our sins, he will forgive our sins. He will forgive every wrong thing we have done. He will make us pure. If we claim we have not sinned, we are calling God a liar. His word is not in us."
1 JOHN 1: 8–10

My Abba,

If your desired mark is your holy bullseye, I realize that sometimes I fail to land my arrow anywhere near the target. I know I sin. I miss your mark.

I think I just want to pretend I am not guilty of sin I consider less palatable. I don't want to admit to the stuff I feel is rank. The three-day-old rotting junk in the trash bin just can't belong to me. I want to see my transgressions as less offensive, more dainty and discreet.

This is a curious attitude that reveals lies I believe about you and me. When I entertain these lies, I am like a preschooler smearing around finger paints thinking I am a better "smearer" than the other kids who smear.

Therefore, by my faulty calculations, I should be admitted to the master's class of artistry. Never mind that there has been only one who has ever made the cut, because you have to make perfect art to get in. My smeary mess is better than the one I made last week, and I think it is definitely better than the kid down the street.

Since you are perfectly holy and cannot collaborate with sin, any sin disqualifies me from an eternal relationship with you. You aren't just better than me. You are perfect and I am not. It is binary. You are in that holy class by yourself. I cannot excel enough to be admitted.

SIN: the Greek word "hamartia" is derived from a technical word used in archery, which literally means, "to miss the mark."

When I work through it like this, I realize my foolishness. But please remind me, on a day-to-day basis, that I don't have what it takes to earn my way into your good graces. I don't deserve to spend forever with you because I am a reasonably nice person who on most days tries hard to hit the target.

> *"I don't deserve to spend forever with you because I am a reasonably nice person who on most days tries hard to hit the target."*

Thank you that although I don't hit the bullseye, you are flawless with a bow and arrow, never miss the mark of perfection, and have taken the shot for me.

I love you,
Mollie

My Child,

You are perfectly acceptable to me because of what Jesus did for you. He paid the full price for your admission into an eternity with me. Because you have received that gift, I have forgiven your sins — all of them — perfectly. As you do life with me, I will convict you of your sin, and will always remain faithful and fair to forgive your sin and cleanse you when you miss the mark.

Remember the scene in *My Fair Lady*, when they were trying to coax Eliza Doolittle into a bath. She clung to her dirty clothes and cried, "I'm a good girl, I am." She didn't see her foul state, so she didn't understand the need for a bath.

Hiding your dirty laundry will never serve you well. I will not force you to accept my cleansing forgiveness. To receive my forgiveness, you have to resist the urge to huddle on top of the soiled stuff declaring, "It's not that dirty!"

As always, I want you to willingly receive what I have for you. My provision is matchless, and my forgiveness will truly set you free!

I love you,
Abba

READ MY LIPS

"A good person produces good things from the treasury of a good heart, and an evil person produces evil things from the treasury of an evil heart. What you say flows from what is in your heart."
LUKE 6:45

"May the words of my mouth and the meditation of my heart be pleasing to you, O Lord, my rock and my redeemer."
PSALM 19:14

My Child,

When you feel scalded by others, sometimes your mouth tries to release the scorching steam that is building in your heart. Expressing yourself can be helpful. But when you're upset and don't come to me before speaking to others, the words that flow from your heart might not play well on the main stage of your life.

Your unsanctified speech can compromise your relationships, and you may wind up with a heart hangover the next morning. You know that sick feeling you get after you calm down and are unsure of all the words you said but regret what you do remember.

I want you to make me your first reach when you are wounded. The stampede of your unbridled words will not chase away your pain. Give me that pain. I will carry it for you. Then, as my Spirit leads you, you can express yourself to others.

Whatever is in your heart determines what you say. Since I am the only one who can truly make your heart good, you need my continuing transformation, in order for the fruit of your lips to be life giving.

I love you,
Abba

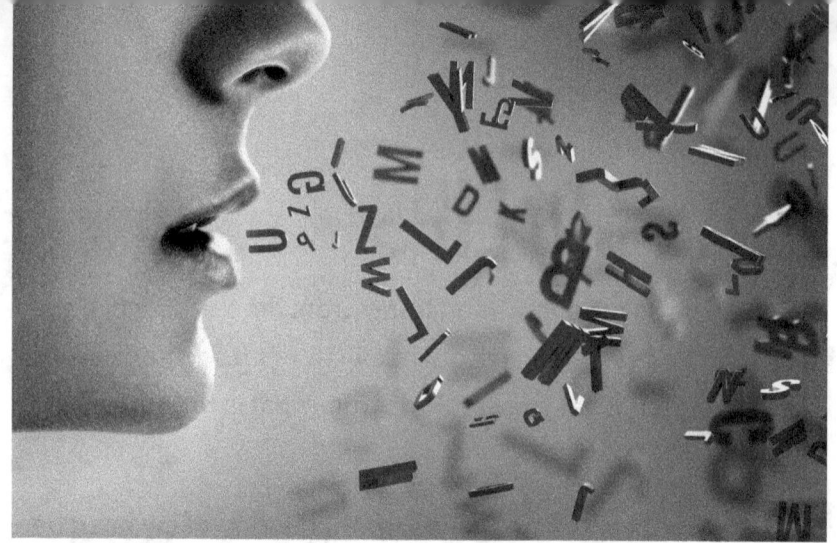

My Abba,

When I perceive something as unjust, I can open my mouth and the rude, the bad, and the ugly may swagger out. I can get swept away in the torrent of my emotions. Sometimes, when I am attempting to make the wrong things right, I get tangled up in my superhero cape as I try to fly in and assume your responsibilities. That scene usually ends in a crash-and-burn routine of some kind.

I want to let your Spirit reign in my heart and mind when I am mad or sad, so that I don't inflict damage and wind up in a swamp of regret. Please be the gatekeeper of my lips as you work to sanctify my thoughts and emotions.

Give me your unconditional love for people. I want to love people when they act in lovable ways, and when they do not. I realize it is not true love, your love, if I only want to "love" someone when they act the way I want them to. I am so thankful you don't love me that way. I am sure I don't look distinctly lovable most of the time. Thank you for loving me despite my significant flaws.

If love is acting in someone else's best interest, then please show me what words will bless others. What words are in their best interest? What words nourish life? May the words on my lips blossom from your tree of life.

I love you,
Mollie

SHIFTING SHADOWS & HEAVENLY LIGHTS

"And remember, when you are being tempted, do not say, 'God is tempting me.' God is never tempted to do wrong, and he never tempts anyone else. Temptation comes from our own desires, which entice us and drag us away. These desires give birth to sinful actions. And when sin is allowed to grow, it gives birth to death. So don't be misled, my dear brothers and sisters. Whatever is good and perfect is a gift coming down to us from God our Father, who created all the lights in the heavens. He never changes or casts a shifting shadow." JAMES 1:13–17

My Abba,

Father of the Heavenly Lights. Another fitting name for you, Beautiful God. I treasure you and your perfect gifts. I love that you never change. No need to worry that you will lose your luster, deteriorate or become irrelevant. Everything else is so inconstant, but you are perfect — always.

Thank you that you are not my tempter. Please alert me to evil desires when they knock on the door of my heart, armed with their smooth sales pitches. I want to cry out to you prior to answering the door. Give me the supernatural sense to reach for you, before I even give my temptation the time of day, much less allow it to entice and drag me away.

I know many of my desires are sacred and from you. But I don't want those that are mangled or misdirected to give birth to sin in my life. And I certainly don't want the death in my life that results

from my sin. One definition I saw for death this morning was this: a damaging or destructive state of affairs. That describes what my sin produces in my life and in the lives of those around me.

Each day I have the opportunity to choose life with you, the Author of Life, or the errant thoughts and behaviors that bring damage and destruction. Please give me the power, Holy Spirit, to choose well today.

I love you,
Mollie

My Child,

Free will (the sacred option for choice) for those I created is a magnificent gift that allows for love. I did not create will-bound puppets without the ability to choose. I wanted the opportunity for a love relationship. Choice and love must go hand in hand.

It is impossible to force someone to love you. That is not love.

The price for this opportunity to love is the opportunity to hate. I don't ever tempt you to hate others or me, or sin against others or me. But the option must be there. One choice cannot be open to you without the other.

*"When you are living deeply in my love,
and temptation knocks,
you will be too involved with me
to answer it."*

    Love is a good and perfect gift I give. But you must choose each day, whether or not, to receive that gift from me. I want to flood your heart with my love today, so you can enjoy loving me and others well.

    When you are living deeply in my love, and temptation knocks, you will be too involved with me to answer it. Leave the shifting shadows outside today, and enjoy being at home with me, reveling in my heavenly light.

I love you,
Abba

THE ART OF REMAINING

"I have loved you even as the Father has loved me. Remain in my love. When you obey my commandments, you remain in my love, just as I obey my Father's commandments and remain in his love. I have told you these things so that you will be filled with my joy. Yes, your joy will overflow!" JOHN 15:9–11

My Abba,

When I look at the meanings of "remain," this truth is so rich. I want to wait in your love. I want to always continue in your unchanging love. I want to be left in your love after everything else has gone. I will continue to need your love after everything else has been dealt with. I want to endure in your love in spite of all challenges.

So, remaining in your love sounds like a perfectly beautiful idea. But then I read the "how to" part, and I am convicted. Words like obey, comply, submit, and command bring me back to reality. You say if I want to remain in your love, I need to obey you. To me, obeying commands does not sound as winsome as remaining in your love.

I don't often associate obedience with joy. My culture tells me I am in charge and should chart my own course. I am told only I can decide what's best for me, and I shouldn't march to anyone else's drum.

Sometimes, I forget you know me infinitely better than I know myself. You are the only consummate expert on me and my best path. You never make poor decisions for me or anyone else.

But when I read verses like the ones I saw this morning in Psalm 119, I know I am not fully embracing truth. My heart is not like the psalmist's.

REMAIN: to wait somewhere; to continue in a particular state without changing; to be left after everything else has gone; to continue to need to be taken care of after everything else has been dealt with; to endure and succeed at continuing on in spite of all   OBEY: comply with the command, direction, or request of; to submit to the authority of; carry out a command or instruction; behave in accordance with

"I have rejoiced in your laws as much as in riches."

"I am always overwhelmed with a desire for
your regulations."

"How I delight in your commands!
How I love them!"

"Your laws are my treasure; they are my
heart's delight."

"I pant with expectation, longing for
your commands."

Psalm 119:14, 20, 47, 111, 131

Please give me joy, delight, desire, love, and longing for your commands, so that I might more consistently enjoy your love. I want your ways to be my treasure.

I love you,
Mollie

My Child,

The reason the psalmist could write about his love for my laws is because he understood they reflected my heart and were flawless.

Your desire to rebel against me and my commands is part of the human experience. Taking pleasure in obedience to my laws is not natural. But I can give you a supernatural desire to please me. My instructions give you a road map but only by my Spirit will you comply joyfully.

Sometimes you don't even consciously decide to defy me. But you let the debris of the day take center stage. When life's clutter rises up incessantly tugging at the hem of your mind, please don't hand it a microphone. I don't want the siren song of your flesh to upstage my plans and purposes for you.

When I ask for obedience to my commands, it is not some cosmic trick I devised to siphon the pleasure right out of your life. As your heart comes into alignment with mine, my joy in you will overflow!

I love you,
Abba

A CONFIDENT APPROACH

"For we do not have a high priest who cannot sympathize with our weaknesses, but One who has been tempted in all things just as we are, yet without sin. Therefore let's approach the throne of grace with confidence, so that we may receive mercy and find grace for help at the time of our need." HEBREWS 4:15–16

My Child,

Jesus was tempted. You definitely will be. The difference is this: He never yielded to temptation. You have and will.

The good news is that Christ knows all about temptation and triumph. If you cry out to him for his power, he will give it to you so that you might resist doing the sinful things you do not have the power to resist without him.

Remember he empathizes with your weaknesses. He fully understands them because he has experienced them.

I have not restricted those who may approach me based on an individual's success with sin management. I do not say, "Some of you good ones may approach." I encourage all who have received the gift of Christ's righteousness to come confidently into my presence.

You don't have to polish your soul before coming. Christ's sacrifice gave you a permanent backstage pass with more privileges than you can imagine. Unfettered access to my throne room has been guaranteed by me, for all time. Whether you feel exceedingly sure-footed or utterly clumsy in your approach, remember, even the most graceful version of yourself is not the source of your confidence. I am.

CONFIDENCE: a feeling of self-assurance arising from one's appreciation of one's own abilities or qualities; a firm trust that one can count on someone or something

My throne is a throne of grace — a glorious place where unearned kindness abounds. Rest in the certainty of that truth. When you depend fully on my grace for your access, you will be assured you can approach me without fear. I cannot mislead you. Deceit is not possible for me.

The path to my presence is not a slippery slope. Come and find joy in my embrace.

I love you,
Abba

My Abba,

I have to trust you to make me right. Pulling myself out of the quicksand of my sin usually results in a lot of flailing and frustration.

I am astounded that Christ was willing to humble himself to the point of experiencing human frailty, temptation, suffering and death. That was not some kind of necessary exercise for your benefit. I know it was all fueled out of your love for us. Thank you for your matchless commitment to our wellbeing.

Through Christ's life, you have demonstrated you have all it takes for us to walk through temptation victoriously. How astounding that you live in me, offer that power to me, and still, I sometimes refuse to take it. Please pour out your power in the weakest parts of my life today and give me the willingness to receive from you.

The definitions of confidence are so telling. One describes a dependence on self, the other a dependence on you. I desire to faithfully depend on you to empower me. I know you have promised me your Holy Spirit lives in me and will give me what I need to resist temptation. But will I choose to ask and receive what I, so obviously, need?

In reality, I vacillate between these two forms of confidence much of the time. When I falsely assume that "I have got this," I have that self-assurance arising from an appreciation of my own abilities. The aftermath of that is never pretty.

Other times I realize rightly that I am powerless apart from you to resist temptation. I have that firm trust that I can, and need, to count on you. I cling to you because I know you are my only hope.

Give me the grace today to choose rightly. I want to put my confidence in you, the Creator of the Universe, not in me, your created one.

I love you,
Mollie

EVERY MOMENT OF FOREVER

"This is a trustworthy saying, and everyone should accept it: 'Christ Jesus came into the world to save sinners'—and I am the worst of them all. But God had mercy on me so that Christ Jesus could use me as a prime example of his great patience with even the worst sinners. Then others will realize that they, too, can believe in him and receive eternal life."
1 TIMOTHY 1:15–16

My Child,

I want you to meditate on this trustworthy saying that deserves full acceptance. Christ came into the world and paid the price for your sin, because I want you to spend every moment of forever with me.

Paul talks about how he was the worst of all sinners. He felt like that, but I actually don't rate sin. You are all on the same playing field. There is no Sinner's A or B team. No good, worst, better, and bad sinners. There is no point system. It is binary in my moral economy. There is perfect. And there is not perfect. I am perfect. You are not.

I know you don't fully understand why the payment for sin is death (eternal absence from my presence). You could comprehend it better if you could truly grasp my perfect holiness. But that is not possible. You will need to trust me on this.

My truth about human sin and my mercy is not trending. I am not fashionable according to the modern ideas of man. I do not morph every time someone changes his, or her, mind about me. The clay does not shape the potter.

Humans want to believe they can climb some imaginary ladder to heaven on their own — one "good deed" rung at a time. But, in reality,

it doesn't work like that. You are sinful like all other humans. Christ was the only exception. He led the perfect life and gave up his life, on your behalf, for your imperfection. His death bought you life. When you accepted his gift of new life, you became part of our family and will live in my perfect presence forever.

I don't love you less because you have shortcomings. My love is eternal, unconditional and flawless. And when my love for you is on display, it shows others more about who I am — unparalleled in patience, grace, and compassion. Take pleasure in these gifts I have given you today.

I love you,
Abba

My Abba,

After all these years, I am still blown away by your faultless love for me. All our human attempts at love are so blemished compared to what you offer.

At times, I find myself tempted to look at my latest performance to see how much you might care for me. The phrase we use, "What have you done for me lately?" sometimes still lurks in my mind. Like you are some fair-weather God who ditches me when I don't perform well. Please forgive me for believing that lie. I know you are perfect in every way. Your forgiveness and love never fail.

Please continue to remind me that you are omnipotent and don't need anything from me. Sometimes I entertain the subtle deception that whispers to me, "Look how people missed out because you didn't step up."

Please ground me in your truth. When I don't participate in your plans and purposes, I am the one who misses out. Not you. Not others. I realize I don't have the power to thwart the God of the Galaxies.

I want to be empowered by your Spirit and active with you today. Not because you need me. But because I need you. And, participating in your kingdom handiwork with you is an unrivaled privilege.

I love you,
Mollie

UNBRIDLED BLISS

Where do I find joy?

THUNDER AND WHISPER

"I will meditate on your majestic, glorious splendor and all your wonderful miracles. Your awe-inspiring deeds will be on every tongue; I will proclaim your greatness."

"They will speak of the glory of your kingdom;
they will give examples of your power"
PSALM 145:5–6, 11

My Abba,

Each day from the time the first fingers of daylight tease the sleepy morning horizon until the moon rests her heavy head in the soft lap of night, your glorious splendor is on display.

Thank you for teaching me to see and celebrate examples of your power. I want to meditate on the wildly delightful things you do — your awe-inspiring ways. I want to see you today for who you are, and live wide awake — contemplating your perfection.

"Keep the flame of my praise kindled as a fragrant offering from a grateful soul."

I love that the word "contemplate" comes from the Latin word "a place for observation." Please help me to enjoy my place for observation with you, as you call to my mind all the extraordinary ways you are working.

Don't let mundane tasks distract me from the mind-blowing epic of your love and grace. The endless demand of dirty dishes, laundry

that seems to reproduce in the utility room, and the menacing pile of paperwork on my desk can steal my attention.

I realize though, even these everyday duties can have eternal value and become an act of celebration, when I invite you to empower me as I do them. When I am doing what you want me to do, dependent on you and your resources, I experience the joy of participating with you, no matter how mundane the activity.

Thank you for reminding me of this truth today. You are an exhilarating companion, whether we dance on breathtaking peaks, in treacherous valleys, or on the broad plains of routine days.

I love you,
Mollie

My Child,

I am glad you want to recognize my miracles in your midst. You can find me at work in the robust and the delicate. The grandest galaxy and smallest atom. The thunder and the whisper.

Many people think the healing of physical disease is the most dramatic evidence of my power. Physical healing is wonderful, but it is only temporary intervention. Everyone's physical body will cease to function at some point.

My glory is shown most powerfully when I transform hearts and souls forever. And when I do, each renewed life becomes a display of my splendor. A sign and symbol of my grace for eternity. I want you to celebrate these transformative miracles with others. Don't get swept up in your next desire without taking time to rejoice in what I have done.

Today, I want you to focus with gratitude on the miracles I have already accomplished in your midst. Think of your family a few years ago. Celebrate the restoration. I am not finished yet, but I don't want you to lose sight of what I have done, as you hunger for more.

Live in celebration today. Keep the flame of my praise kindled as a fragrant offering from a grateful soul.

I love you,
Abba

THE PARTY NEVER ENDS

"Eat them (sacred meals) there with your children, your servants, and the Levites who live in your town, celebrating the presence of the Lord your God in all you do." DEUTERONOMY 12:18b

"With music and singing we celebrate your mighty acts."
PSALM 21:13b

My Abba,

I wonder how differently I would live if each day I found ways to celebrate your presence. I know celebration doesn't mean just throwing a party. (Although, throwing a party for you sounds awesome.)

When I think of the meaning of celebrating, I see it is also about honoring, remembering, recognizing, or commemorating someone who is important — praising publicly or paying tribute to someone.

> *"I want to celebrate your mighty acts with unabashed zeal."*

The idea of celebrating you by praising you publicly reminds me of the way the shepherds responded to their encounter with Jesus in the film I watched the other night called *The Chosen*. No one had to prod them into expressing their joy.

They bounded around town broadcasting their good news to every man, woman, child and donkey in Bethlehem. These ecstatic messengers brought the party to the public square.

I want to celebrate your mighty acts with unabashed zeal. If possible, I want to be guilty of over-sharing how awesome you are.

CELEBRATE: publicly acknowledge with a social gathering or enjoyable activity, to honor or praise publicly

I want to start indulging in a daily joy-filled celebration of you. Please fuel my adventure to celebrate you.

I love you,
Mollie

My Child,

Most people don't think I am the partying kind. But I invented the idea! The Holy Spirit, Son and I are always celebrating. We celebrate each other, all we created, love, peace, joy, righteousness, beauty, truth, faithfulness and every other good thing.

What joy would be yours if you lived every day in celebration of who I am and what I do! As you get to know me better, you will find, even, more ways to celebrate me.

Think about how you celebrate a loved one's birthday and certain practices will come to mind. You might write a note highlighting the qualities you admire in him or her — the attributes that make them one-of-a-kind. You might try to find a gift that expresses your love. You might attend a party in his or her honor. You might tell others what you appreciate about that person.

Those practices are also ways you can celebrate me. When you write to me expressing your love, you celebrate me. When you share with others gifts I have given you, you celebrate me. (That is the ultimate practice of "re-gifting.") When you gather with your forever family in my name, you celebrate me. Whenever you tell others about your love for me, you celebrate me.

And by the way, you do throw parties for me. Each time you help create an event to acknowledge, celebrate or praise me, it is a party and I am the honoree.

Those celebrations are a taste of eternity. My road does go on forever, and my party never, ever ends!

I love you,
Abba

OASIS

"Yes, the Lord has done amazing things for us. What joy!" PSALM 126:3

My Abba,

The past week, we have waded shoulder deep in the waters of temporal blessing. You have done great things for us. I want to be jubilant like the psalmist exclaiming, "What joy!"

But even as I thank you for this gift, I feel an awkward undercurrent of discomfort with this comfort. I want to enjoy the pleasure of these refreshing springs. But I realize I need your power to do that.

As I write this, it sounds so bizarre and ungrateful. Why do I need your power to enjoy something so enjoyable? Why am I uncomfortable taking pleasure in the material gift you have given us? Honestly, I feel self-indulgent and guilty. The weight of this temporal blessing is throwing off my spiritual and emotional equilibrium.

I want to walk well with you in pleasure and pain. I want to enjoy all circumstantial and spiritual blessings. But I realize I need your grace on every path — the brutal and the beautiful. I know how to find joy in your matchless presence in the midst of chronic pain, abuse, and devastating loss.

You, your beauty, and magnificent spiritual blessings have carried me through so many battles in my life. So here we are. The trials have not evaporated. Empowered by your Spirit, I am still in the ring swinging wildly at heartbreak, chronic pain, broken family connections, Parkinson's, and the cobwebs of abuse.

I often say, "We can enjoy God's presence in the midst of any circumstance." But honestly, I was only thinking of the truly difficult ones dealing knockout punches.

You are always my beautiful Respite. Whether I am up against the ropes under a barrage of blows, or experiencing peace and protection

from my opponents, please show me how to be increasingly captivated by you.

I love you,
Mollie

My Child,

Yes, you have had a lot of practice walking with me in pain. You have enjoyed intimate communion with me in the midst of a deluge of adversity. But just because I have brought something pleasant in your life, does not mean our relationship will wither.

You are leery because struggle is what you know. It is familiar. You have wrestled with trauma as long as you can remember. And in your struggle, you allowed me to carry you. Out of the ashes of your life, you let me nourish in you a glorious dependence on me.

That is why you believe this "amazing thing" might hinder our relationship. You are afraid it might weaken our connection, if you aren't desperate for my presence in order to take your next breath. But pleasure in circumstantial blessings does not change reality. Your deepest joy is still found in me. No pain or pleasure can ever alter that.

Your dependence on me is not dependent on difficult or delightful circumstances. You have trusted me to grow our connection as we walked through the valley of the shadow of death. Now trust me to cause our communion to flourish in this oasis, also.

I love you,
Abba

WAKING TO WONDER

"Everyone was gripped with great wonder and awe, and they praised God, exclaiming, 'We have seen amazing things today!'" LUKE 5:26

My Child,

Your worship makes me smile. You are enjoying what you were created for — celebrating the wonder of knowing me. I want you to always remember the joy you are experiencing now.

Don't forfeit this joy for anything or anyone else. Don't trade what is enduring, pure and imperishable for what will disappear faster than all those presents dressed in festive wrap under your Christmas tree.

Remember that empty ache you sense after all the earthly trappings of the holidays are over. That is how passing pleasure works — promising you the sun and moon but delivering the light of a flickering match that will soon be snuffed out.

The joy you find in me will not quiver and can never be extinguished. Every morning I want you to wake to a glorious beginning, wrapped in my tender mercies, as you are transformed into a vibrant instrument of my praise.

I want your life to sing of my mercy, faithfulness, love and grace. I want your life to sing of my beauty, holiness, kindness and goodness. I want my music to play so deeply in your heart that the unmistakable melody of my ardent love will echo in the hearts of those around you.

I love you,
Abba

WONDER: *a feeling of surprise mingled with admiration, caused by something beautiful, unexpected, unfamiliar, or inexplicable*

My Abba,

I want to wake each morning to this immeasurable pleasure of being with you. Right now, the delight you are pouring into me makes me feel like I will break open.

I do not have any words that seem fitting to respond to your love. I am so grateful you can witness the overwhelming joy you have created in my love-steeped heart. Right now, that is all I have to offer.

This life is hard and crazy. I don't want to do the hard and crazy without you. I would not want to wake up at all, if that were all there was.

But your mercies are new every morning. I wake and nothing about you lost its luster during the night. You are still gloriously perfect in every way.

You are a matchless, loyal companion. Your unswerving devotion to me changes my perception of everything around me. Even when life is excruciating, you don't discard me to be devoured by the pain.

Your life-giving presence brings me inextinguishable joy. Thank you that we are inseparable. Thank you that I am forever yours. I love being loved by you.

I want to see your beauty, even before I open my eyes each morning. Please make me increasingly sensitive to who you are.

Let me enjoy you in new ways today. Surprise me! I want to be a child wowed by the wonders of knowing you.

I love you,
Mollie

SEE AND BE GLAD

"The humble will see their God at work and be glad. Let all who seek God's help be encouraged." PSALM 69:32

"You must have the same attitude that Christ Jesus had. Though he was God, he did not think of equality with God as something to cling to. Instead, he gave up his divine privileges; he took the humble position of a slave and was born as a human being." PHILIPPIANS 2:5–7

My Abba,

I know many people think that being humble means to have a "low estimate of one's own importance." But I sense there may be a better understanding of humility as I read verses like those in Philippians.

Christ did not live the life he did because he was clueless about his status as God and had a low estimate of his importance. He was fully aware of his deity. He had an accurate view of himself.

He didn't try to convince people he was less than the Creator of all. But though he acknowledged his station, he did not choose to cling to his privileges. He became a servant to those he created. These thoughts give me a better sense of how to practice humility in my own life.

I don't think you want me to live in a state of constant self-deprecation. It has taken me many years to see myself as a valued child of the King. But I do think as I follow Christ, you call me to not grasp at things to which I might think I am entitled.

When I get a clearer vision of who you are and who I am, I sense I am walking in humility. It is a simple recognition that you are God and I am not. I want to see the beautiful miracles you are performing all around me. I want to give credit where credit is due. I don't want to miss the splendor of your sunrise. Please give me a front row seat to watch what you are up to.

As I see you and me with greater clarity, I become increasingly aware of the truth of us. The reality of our relationship is shocking and captivating at the same time. Your love exposes the lies I have believed about you and me.

Thank you for allowing me to see my God at work and be glad!

I love you,
Mollie

My Child,

There is a simple reason why the humble will see me at work and be glad. When your hands are busy trying to commandeer situations to put yourself first, raise your prestige, point to your achievements and give yourself the credit, you are too busy to notice what my hands are actually doing. Gratitude never has a chance to take root.

The first step is to actually recognize the gifts I am giving out of my love for you. The next step is to embrace the truth that they are not wages — something you earned and are owed. When you acknowledge that I don't owe you anything but choose to give relentlessly, then a grateful heart can grow. Nourishing an attitude of gratitude pushes out pride.

It is not demeaning or degrading to respectfully submit to me. In reality, it will make your heart glad. The world may tell you all submission is soul robbery. That is not true when it comes to submitting to me.

I created you to yield to me. I am the only one with perfect plans. No matter how many talents I have given you or how hard you work, you cannot top perfection. If you really tune into what I am doing, it will make your heart sing. Watch the amazing ways I work to create life, transform the human heart, redeem pain, change the course of history, bring order from chaos, and beauty from ashes.

I am God of the Galaxies and beyond. Everything good, perfect, infinite and eternal is from me — including the good in you! Bask in the beauty of my goodness today and live in joy.

I love you,
Abba

UNBRIDLED BLISS

"Each time he said, 'My grace is all you need.
My power works best in weakness.'
So now I am glad to boast about my weaknesses,
so that the power of Christ can work through me."
2 CORINTHIANS 12:9

My Abba,

Since Gracie's sudden departure to heaven last weekend, emotional shock waves continue to roll in breaking our hearts and leveling our equilibrium. We are left with a gaping hole in our hearts that will never be totally filled this side of heaven.

As I reflect on Gracie's life and homecoming, her life verse impacts me in an even greater way. She spent her whole life in an extremely weak place if you evaluate her time on earth from a cognitive and physical perspective. I am still blown away when I think about how Gracie entered this world with Down's syndrome, fought the most aggressive form of leukemia at age two, and sustained a severe brain injury by age three that left her fully dependent.

Since your power works best in weakness, it is no wonder Gracie was such a radiant display of your power. In her frailty, there was ample space for you to reveal your extravagant presence. I am also convinced she had the benefit of enjoying a preview of heaven at three when she had no heartbeat for 20 minutes. I think she saw glorious things she simply could not un-see.

Although Gracie returned to us without language we could clearly understand, she never needed words to worship you. After her experience with you "outside" her body, Gracie's exquisite response to even the mention of your name was unbridled bliss.

If we prayed or worshiped in her presence, Gracie brought a whole new meaning to the spiritual practice of "ecstatic utterance." She always celebrated you like no one was looking. That is the greatest gift

she gave me. Gracie was a woman who worshiped you with her whole being and was unashamed.

Your grace was definitely all she needed. When I read the words I wrote above describing Gracie as "fully dependent," I realize those words describe so much more than her physical condition. She was fully dependent on you.

I want to be more like Gracie. I want to be fully dependent on you, experiencing the unbridled bliss of your presence. In my utter weakness, please be my boundless Strength.

I love you,
Mollie

My Child,

Even my Son experienced the sting of a loved one's physical death when his friend Lazarus died. Though Jesus knew he would raise Lazarus from the grave, he still wept.

I created my beloved ones with a desire for eternal connection with each other and me. I did not design you for this grievous separation. It feels wrong for a reason.

I know you do not grieve as one without hope. You clearly anticipate a magnificent reunion someday with Gracie and other loved ones who have gone before you. But I expect your sorrow now. I will carry you through the anguish. Your pain, no matter how consuming, is no rival for my comfort.

Remember, Gracie's light has not gone out. I shone through her in a supernatural way. I will continue to use her. My light can never be extinguished. Always rejoice in the memories of her luminous presence. And realize you can't come close to imagining the way she now shines as she sees me face to face.

This life will soon be past. Live like Gracie did. Enamored with my presence and overflowing with contagious joy.

I love you,
Abba

THE KINDNESS OF CONVICTION

How does God make me more like him?

WHAT ARE YOU DRINKING?

"Don't you see how wonderfully kind, tolerant, and patient God is with you? Does this mean nothing to you? Can't you see that his kindness is intended to turn you from your sin?" ROMANS 2:4

My Child,

I don't want you to sin. I desire only what is good for you. Sin is not. I want you to imagine two water sources. While they both may look fine for drinking, one is pure, delicious water and the other is polluted.

One problem with polluted water is that it may, or may not, look polluted. You also may not fully grasp the adverse effects until much later. I can see what will happen down the road if you drink the polluted water of this world. It may depend on how contaminated it is or how often you drink it. But anything other than my living water will have a negative impact at some level — at some point.

If you choose the tainted water, it will sadden me because it is not my best for you. But I have made provision for those times. Christ is your advocate who lived a perfect life and gave it up to pay for the poor choices of his loved ones. He also came to demonstrate how to choose well. He always chose the pure living water of my love.

The delight I offer you arises from the wellspring of my kindness. Drink and see I am good!

I love you,
Abba

My Abba,

It is absurd that I ever see your invitation of life as a set of needless restrictions that burdens me, depriving me of pleasure. I have chased after so many things that promised pleasure but were polluted.

Now as a parent and grandparent, I can imagine what it would be like to buy, at great cost, a beautiful, pristine, spring-fed stream for my children and grandchildren to have a healthy source of water. What if I encouraged them daily to drink from those waters, but they kept trying to satisfy their thirst at a bacteria-infested, muddy livestock pond, instead?

> *"Let me follow you to your river of delights!"*

It would break my heart because I would know they would eventually get sick. I would do everything I could to stop them. I can imagine how devastated I would feel if they drank the dirty water anyway.

What if despite my sacrificial provision for them, they saw me as demanding, narrow-minded, and controlling? What if despite my love for them, they thought I was ruining their lives by trying to get them to do something they desperately needed, but didn't want to do?

If I, as an imperfect parent with finite love, would feel that deep pain, I can grasp (in a small way) the sadness it brings you when I choose dirty water. Please enlighten my heart and help me choose your living water today.

Let me follow you to your river of delights!

I love you,
Mollie

AT HOME

"Jesus answered him, 'If anyone loves me, he will keep my word, and my Father will love him, and we will come to him and make our home with him. Whoever does not love me does not keep my words. And the word that you hear is not mine but the Father's who sent me.'" JOHN 14: 23–24

My Child,

As your love grows for me, your desire to keep my word will flourish also. More and more, you will want to do what I ask you to. This happens because as our relationship grows, your trust in me blossoms. When you believe my way is best, you are more prone to demonstrate that by following my directions.

Remember I have the perfect perspective that you lack. You cannot see things from my eternal vantage point. What seems foolish to you may actually be wise. You just can't see everything, all the time, and process it flawlessly, like I can.

Since we (the Son, Spirit, and I) have made our home with you, our living arrangement has changed you. We love being with you. You are increasingly experiencing the joy of our glorious communion. Rely on my Spirit to teach you and give you the desire and power to follow me. Even when things look wild and crazy out there, we can give you everything you need to thrive.

Don't let your problems consume you. I want you to be caught up in my larger-than-life, transcendent, eternal, overarching story. There is so much more happening than what you can see, touch, hear, and chew on. Trust me on this. I have been around the block more than a few times. Nothing surprises me.

I love you,
Abba

My Abba,

I have been thinking about how "impractical" keeping your word can seem from the human perspective. It doesn't always seem practical to abide by certain rules or laws. It doesn't always seem practical to do what you say is right when "no one" is looking. It doesn't always seem practical to beat back our busyness to spend time with you. There is so much to do.

But the more I get to know you and the more consistent our communication becomes, the more I realize it does not always have to make sense to me. You are not under some kind of obligation to give me all the answers. I need to embrace the fact that your mind and mine are infinitely different when it comes to perspective. I am only seeing a tiny piece of your eternal timeline from a very limited vantage point. It seems comical when I really think about it.

If a toddler in the last row of a massive football stadium were watching the Super Bowl, would we find it appropriate for him to make the call that would decide the game? But I stand on my little speck of ground in the universe, time-bound, and influenced by my sin nature and think I know definitively how things should go down. I am sorry for my poor judgment. Please forgive me.

I certainly love the idea of you making your home with me. I know how those with whom we live influence us. They bring their preferences, rhythms, habits, priorities, passions and perspectives. They substantially influence our environment.

So what about you taking up residence with me? I want you to set the tone for our environment. I don't want to flee the home front when you disrupt business as usual. You always make our home better. I lose sight of that at times. Please show me how to enjoy being at home with you today.

Permeate my heart, our home, with your presence!

I love you,
Mollie

LIVING LOVE

"If anyone claims, 'I am living in the light,' but hates a fellow believer, that person is still living in darkness. Anyone who loves a fellow believer is living in the light and does not cause others to stumble. But anyone who hates a fellow believer is still living and walking in darkness. Such a person does not know the way to go, having been blinded by the darkness."
1 JOHN 2:9–11

My Abba,

I don't want to be hobbled by even a remnant of hate, that may be shrouded in the shadows of my wounded soul. Cleanse me of any malice, which might covertly breed in the hidden crevices of my heart. I don't want to stumble, or cause others to stumble, by dwelling in the dark caves of subtle hostility.

I want to truly walk, talk, think, and act, like your child. I want the family resemblance to be clearly visible. I want to have some qualities that remind others, in some way, of your traits, your characteristics.

More than anything else, I want to resemble you in the way you love. Please pour out your love through me to the ones in my life who are difficult to love. Empower me to love the "unlovelies" well.

Sometimes, I am prone to show "love" to difficult people by giving into their wishes, even when that is not in their best interest. I realize that is not authentic love. Your love does not act like a doormat to keep the peace. You are never a doormat, and I know you want me to emulate you in all things. Please continually show me how to speak the truth in love, act in love, and pray in love. I want to be a radiant child who lives in the light defined by your love.

*"I want to be a radiant child
who lives in the light
defined by your love."*

In the midst of this current rush of relational pain, I pray I could love my offenders well. Please show me what that looks like. Once again, I give the pain to you. Saturate my heart with your love today, my beautiful Father.

I love you,
Mollie

My Child,

Yes, you need the power of my Spirit to love your enemies. That is not something you can tackle with enough focus, muscle and determination. When the choices of your enemies mangle your dreams, you are turning to me more and more. That is good.

But I also would encourage you to look to me for the unconditional love you need to truly love those you care about the most. You may be tempted to believe you can love the lovable ones well on your own.

But why would you want to shortchange the ones you care about so deeply? If your enemies deserve my love poured out through you, don't you also want that expression of love for those who are most precious to you?

Ask me for my supernatural love in those relationships as well. I can love them through you with an infinite, perfect, endless love. No matter how deeply you care for someone, my love is not something you can create apart from me.

My love is immeasurable, without flaw and without end. Let me empower you to love with my love, whether it is directed toward your dearest relation or worst enemy.

I love you,
Abba

POWER TO CLING

"But we are looking forward to the new heavens and new earth he has promised, a world filled with God's righteousness. And so, dear friends, while you are waiting for these things to happen, make every effort to be found living peaceful lives that are pure and blameless in his sight. And remember, our Lord's patience gives people time to be saved."
2 PETER 3:13–15a

My Abba,

Thank you that you endure all our failings and love us still. Thank you for your patience. Since most of us are not living peaceful lives that are pure and blameless in your sight, relationships can be pretty challenging. Sometimes I feel like I am trying to run a race with high hurdles, while continually busting my kneecaps on one hurdle after another. I want you to make all things right, new and beautiful — today.

But thank you that while we wait, you are drawing people into eternal relationships with you. That is worth everything — even a painful race to the finish line.

I want to understand more about what "pure and blameless" looks like in my life. I know you have made me pure and blameless eternally by Christ's sacrifice. But what does it look like to walk that out day by day? I want to exhibit now outward evidence of my eternal inner transformation.

My mouth seems to be the point of greatest spiritual contention. A tenacious battle persists for control of that territory. I realize I have the power to build up, or tear down, others with my words. I want you to be victorious in my speech.

Whatever is in my heart overflows in my speech. My mouth remains my faithful informant. It keeps me in touch with the realities of my heart. I thank you for that. My mouth tells me the truth about

where I am with you. When my heart is polluted, I spit sewage. When my heart is dry, I spit sand. (Neither option is attractive.)

Please transform me. When your living water refreshes me, I am privileged to be a conduit for your life-giving flow. That is what I want to be. In that place, I experience the great joy of being the vessel you designed me to be.

I love you,
Mollie

My Child,

You cannot imagine the glories of the new heaven and earth I have planned. Your keenest imagination is only a spark in the dark. This vapor of your present life is not all there is.

I want the suffering to stop, too. But despite my desire to relieve all temporal pain on earth, the priority of establishing eternal connection between my people and me is much more crucial. I know sometimes it doesn't feel that way when pain has you, and those you love, in a chokehold.

The only way to thrive in this life is to cling with all you are to all I am. (And I can give you the power to cling. Just ask.)

"I will hold onto you, whether you are quietly clinging to me or wildly flailing."

You never expected your babies to cling to you unaided. You held them as they tried to hold onto you. Even when they arched their backs and thrashed about, you didn't drop them. In my perfect strength, I will hold onto you, whether you are quietly clinging to me or wildly flailing.

I am pure, unending Life — Love, Joy, and Peace. Don't believe the world peddling lies with haughty confidence. True life with limitless love, joy and peace is not found in anyone else's arms.

Cling to me today. I will cling to you. The rest is details.

I love you,
Abba

THE KINDNESS OF CONVICTION

"for our gospel did not come to you in word only, but also in power and in the Holy Spirit and with full conviction; just as you know what kind of men we proved to be among you for your sakes."
1 THESSALONIANS 1:5

My Child,

You are bombarded with confusion from your culture, especially when it comes to the difference between conviction and condemnation. Many people don't grasp the idea that when you are guilty of an offense, my conviction is a healthy part of being in relationship with me.

Once someone has come into relationship with me through Christ, there is no condemnation. I simply offer forgiveness as you agree with me about your sin. Shame and condemnation are not productive and attack the person while screeching he or she is unfit. Conviction, on the other hand, is productive and moves people toward the truth and greater life in me.

Think about your grandson. Those who love him want to move him toward the truth about what is healthy, right, and good. You would not allow him to wander off the edge of a cliff because he wanted to or did not know better. You would not be shaming him if you took action to

---

CONVICTION: a formal declaration that someone is guilty, the quality of showing that one is firmly convinced of what one believes or says. GUILT: the fact of having committed an offense SHAME: painful feeling of humiliation or disgrace, a feeling of loss of respect or esteem, a feeling of inadequacy or dishonor, a perception that someone or something has no value or worth CONDEMNATION: expression of complete disapproval of someone, typically in public, officially declared to be unfit for use

show him that behavior is wrong — not what is best for him. It would not be controlling, legalistic, and shaming for you to tell him jumping off the cliff was not good behavior.

I know how utterly destructive sin is. I want so much more for my children. I want you to enjoy the life I created for you in all its glory. When you choose poorly, you miss out.

My priority is to establish a forever connection with those I created and love. I hate anything that gets in the way. I work to convict you (convince you of the truth) about those things. I don't do it because I want to ruin your quality of life. I AM LIFE. I want to free you to enjoy me and the abundant life for which you were created.

I love you,
Abba

My Abba,

When a building is condemned, I realize it doesn't just mean it is officially declared "unfit for use." It means that building, either, can't be restored or isn't worth it. It needs to be torn down, leveled, destroyed.

I am so grateful you don't see me that way. Your endless, perfect grace can always bring restoration in my heart, mind and life. Thank you that you don't condemn me. Instead, you always love me unconditionally, and invest lavishly in the astounding transformation of my soul.

You offered me an eternal, vital connection with you through Jesus Christ. Because of that, I can rest assured I am not worthless, condemned, or declared unfit. I can be shame-free, not because I am sin-free, but because you gave me Jesus's perfect, infinite righteousness when I trusted him as my Savior.

Shame tells me, "You are bad, unfit, dirty! Sit in your pain. You deserve to suffer." Conviction says, "Your attitude or action was wrong. Go to God, admit it, receive his forgiveness, and experience the freedom only he can give. Then you can enjoy his best for you."

Thank you for giving me a greater ability to discern between the voices of shame and conviction. Please rescue me from the accuser whenever he attempts to bury me in condemnation. And please convict me when I am actually guilty of an offense, so I may come to you for forgiveness, freedom and life.

I love you,
Mollie

GOD'S GREEN THUMB

"I am the true grapevine, and my Father is the gardener. He cuts off every branch of mine that doesn't produce fruit, and he prunes the branches that do bear fruit so they will produce even more." JOHN 15:1–2

My Abba,

I do want to be more fruitful. I want to imagine myself as a thriving branch on the prolific fig tree nestled in the bend of our backyard fence. Vivid green leaves play in the gusty spring breeze and supple branches brim with countless ripening figs.

But I have to admit I am not enamored with the idea of you shaping me with your cosmic pruning shears. I have lived long enough to know the pruning process is not all sunshine and fun. I don't feel an overwhelming desire to rush to the front of the line for pruning.

But as I said, I still want to be a vigorous branch loaded with the fruit of your Spirit. How can I reconcile my desire to walk, talk, and look more like you with my desire to skip the process of pruning?

I want you to work in and through me, even if you have to remove "superfluous or unwanted parts," in order "to increase my fruitfulness and growth." Please give me courage. By the power of your Holy Spirit, grow me up (make me more fruitful). I am powerless to transform myself.

I know I must abide in you in order for you to do your good work in me. I don't want to hide and wither. Please keep me flourishing and vital as I remain in you, a branch well connected, pruned and nourished.

I love you,
Mollie

PRUNE: to cut away dead or overgrown branches or stems, especially to increase fruitfulness and growth, to remove superfluous or unwanted parts

My Child,

Apart from me, you can do no good that exceeds the limits of your own strength. I don't want your humanity to fence you in. I want to empower you to shatter the boundaries of your flesh-and-blood potential.

I have made you for greater things. And through my power, you can flourish in ways you did not consider possible.

Every time you conquer that seemingly invincible summit ... every time you choose to give me that swarming pain that threatens to swallow your soul ... every time you forgive what seems unforgivable ... every time you give up a passing pleasure to walk with me into something glorious and eternal ... it is because you have allowed me to give you what you need to exceed the limits of your own strength. You are practicing my version of willpower (your willingness to depend on my power).

The apple tree does not have to strain to produce ripe, crisp apples. The grape vine doesn't grit its teeth to produce delicious, juicy grapes. The cherry tree does not struggle to produce mouth-watering cherries. But if the gardener provides protection, good soil, nourishment, water, pruning, and light, the outcome will be a more abundant harvest. You can bear wondrous, supernatural fruit, if you trust me as your gardener.

I know what you need to flourish. You are a finite, created being. But you are also an eternal vessel where my Spirit resides. Let me tend the garden of your heart. I have the ultimate green thumb. You will be overwhelmed with the harvest.

I love you,
Abba

LOVE LAWS

"So Christ has truly set us free. Now make sure that you stay free, and don't get tied up again in slavery to the law."

"But we who live by the Spirit eagerly wait to receive by faith the righteousness God has promised to us."
GALATIANS 5:1, 5

My Abba,

I am so grateful for your rescue! Thank you for setting this captive free. Today I want to celebrate the freedom you have given me. You released me from the tyranny of my captor and gave me a life I could have never envisioned.

My adventure with you has not prevented heartbreak, blisters, and scars. But I would not trade my journey with you, for any other without you.

Cause me to increasingly treasure my liberty. When I lose sight of what you have done for me, I can overlook the beauty of your dazzling rescue. Sometimes my former captor still tries to whisper subtle lies about the luxuries he could offer inside his gilded cage. I am grateful that you dispel his dark strategies with your light.

> *"I would not trade my journey with you, for any other without you."*

Thank you for giving me the freedom to obey your laws. I don't want to worship your rules. But please give me everything I need to see my obedience as an act of worship — a way to say thank you for what you have done for me.

I know I will never be made right in your sight by obedience to my best-dressed holy scheme. That two-ton, self-righteous albatross would take me under. I don't want to live life gasping for my next

virtuous breath, trying to be good enough to make the cut. I want to be that child who rests peacefully on the surface of life's waters, kept afloat by the perfect buoyancy of your grace.

Through the power of your Holy Spirit, I want to become more like you. Not because I have to, in order to be yours. But because I want to, since I am yours.

I love you,
Mollie

My Child,

You don't have to live like your life with me depends on your flawless service record. That is not reality. But you won't want to miss out on the life I have for you.

Don't let our enemy sell you on the delusion that my plans for you will compromise your best life. He is only interested in your death.

I did not craft spiteful commandments to make my children miserable and then open the hatch of heaven to pour them on your heads, burying you in the rubble of legalism. You are mine, so you are free! You are free to enjoy me, walk with me, and glorify me forever.

Now, you can choose to obey my love laws because of your love and gratitude for me. Out of my love for you, I gave them to you. Out of your love for me, I want you to live by them.

My ways are life giving, not joy snatching. Even when my methods seem upside-down to you, trust me. As you walk within the boundaries of my principles, you will find all the freedom you are looking for.

I love you,
Abba

EXPOSED THORNS

How do I survive the heartbreak?

LIMPING HOME

"So be truly glad. There is wonderful joy ahead, even though you must endure many trials for a little while."
1 PETER 1:6

My Abba,

I need your grace to breathe. My wounded heart is howling plaintively about the struggle. I acknowledge the pain. I realize I can't bring sorrow to you that I refuse to admit is harassing me and threatening my joy. As I face the reality of my adversity, I am desperate for you.

Apart from you, my joy shrivels. I know this has always been true, but as time passes, I have become exquisitely sensitive to that reality. The more my powerlessness is unmasked, the more obvious my need for your power becomes.

I know you see my life as a morning mist. Here this morning and gone this afternoon. But when I am in enough pain, seconds can feel like hours. Days feel like months. This life does not feel like "a little while."

Please let me experience your perfect grace, whether I have blistered feet and sand in my teeth trudging through a scorching desert, or I am enjoying a cool summer breeze as I float down a sparkling mountain stream. You are glorious no matter where I am. I know it is an honor to carry that glory in some small way, even if I limp all the way to heaven.

Please strengthen me with your endless comfort, love and peace. I want to delight in your presence today. I want my life to reflect you in a way that draws fellow travelers to you, no matter what the terrain might be.

I love you,
Mollie

My Child,

Sometimes you feel like you will crumble under the weight of your physical and emotional challenges. I know you are weary of the pain, illness, and fatigue.

But even when I don't give you a free pass on pain, I am eternally committed to you. I made my home in you. Our spirits are inextricably knitted together. I am holding you, even, when you feel you are free-falling into a bottomless chasm spiked with trials.

"You have the privilege of living life with a limp."

You have the privilege of living life with a limp. You can choose to live in a way that demonstrates I am more than enough to sustain you. Your story carries weight with those who know you because they realize life has not been a leisurely stroll at the seashore for you.

Your trials give you more opportunities to share how my power sustains you. If you had spent all of your days traversing powder puff trails, how could you share the ways I have carried you through the valley of the shadow of death?

You have fresh opportunities each day to be a conduit of my love, power, grace and forgiveness. I, the God of the Universe, chose you to be an image bearer of my glory. I will continue to show you what a matchless honor that is. Revel in my grace and love as we share this adventure together today.

I love you,
Abba

SAVOR THE SIP

"Jesus replied, 'Anyone who drinks this water will soon become thirsty again. But those who drink the water I give will never be thirsty again. It becomes a fresh, bubbling spring within them, giving them eternal life.'

"'Please, sir,' the woman said, 'give me this water! Then I'll never be thirsty again, and I won't have to come here to get water.'" JOHN 4:13–15

My Abba,

Thank you for understanding my physical, emotional, intellectual, and spiritual needs and frailties. You know them better than I do, because you have perfect knowledge, created me, and made your home in me. I am so grateful nothing is hidden from you.

You are perfectly acquainted with every cell in my body, every emotion in my heart, and every thought in my mind. You see my thirst for so many things. Even though I drink, you know I will soon become thirsty again.

It comforts me to remember you are not some detached spiritual force that cannot relate to my struggles. I am glad you have the most intimate knowledge of all my desires and me.

The woman at the well wanted her physical thirst to be sated permanently. I can relate. Her request resonates with me, "Please, sir, give me this water!"

Sometimes life can leave me desperately yearning for relief. It feels like my tongue is so completely stuck to the roof of my mouth I don't know how to swallow. When I ask for you to relieve that circumstantial thirst (need or want), I admit, in my flesh, I am disappointed if I don't get the quick magic-wand fix.

"Satisfy me with an endless cup of fresh spring water from your eternal fountain of delights."

    Since it is not your way to run around preventing all my discomfort, I need you to refresh my perspective. Many times, what you offer me is something living and eternal instead. It might be patience, trust, joy, love, wisdom, strength, or peace in the midst of what troubles me. Please increase my passion for the inexhaustible well of your presence, especially, in the midst of a "parched and weary land where there is no water."*

    Satisfy me with an endless cup of fresh spring water from your eternal fountain of delights. Please capture my heart today with your eternal pleasure that never runs dry.

I love you,
Mollie

* PSALM 63:1

My Child,

Even in the face of scorching circumstances that threaten to shrivel your soul, I can bring you a supernatural sip of life. Nothing can replace, compete with, or snatch that away.

No perfectly crafted situation according to your desire du jour, no rose garden waltz through this life, no completion of the ultimate bucket list will ever trump the experience of wading shoulder deep in the glory of my living water.

That eternal experience is what you were made for. You are an eternal creature in a temporal tent passing through this earthbound chapter of your life. Your tent has to be maintained and your responsibilities tended to while you are on earth, but they are not who you are. Eternal creatures are only truly satisfied by what is eternal.

I am the delightful, everlasting spring within you. The blistering droughts of this life can never overwhelm me. Only I can satisfy your deepest, abiding thirst. Be refreshed in me, your Living Water! Savor a sip of eternity today.

I love you,
Abba

EXPOSED THORNS

"Yes, and everyone who wants to live a godly life in Christ Jesus will suffer persecution."
2 TIMOTHY 3:12

My Abba,

This is not a verse quoted often by Christians who want to live healthy and wealthy in a well-tended rose garden. Believers who live in relative "safety" are prone to think of persecution as something limited to what evil people do to our brothers and sisters in faraway countries.

Or in a broader sense, we think of cruelty perpetrated on those with less power because of religion, race, class or gender. But this says, "everyone who wants to live a godly life in Christ Jesus will suffer persecution."

> *"Thank you for never abandoning me in the heat of the battle."*

Although there definitely seem to be seasons and regions where persecution is relentless and dire, I don't think our enemy only harasses those in openly oppressive countries. I think he uses, not just humans, but disease, devastation, abuse, and many other losses as he persecutes those who love you. I believe he can treat all those who truly commit to you with hostility, persistently annoying and harassing us.

This truth helps me make more sense of my life. Sometimes my circumstances just seem stifling and aggravating like the feel of coarse wool stuck to hot, sweaty skin. Other times though, life can feel excruciating as in, "I don't think I can draw another breath with

---

PERSECUTION: hostility and ill-treatment, especially because of race or political or religious beliefs, persistent annoyance or harassment

this knife in my belly." But I have experienced the transcendent, unrivaled gift of your presence in all those moments. Thank you for never abandoning me in the heat of the battle.

Please give me everything I need to live for you in the midst of persecution. Because thorns can grow everywhere, even in a rose garden.

I love you,
Mollie

My Child,

Our enemy is an equal opportunity oppressor. He does not restrict his persecution of the saints to those in specific times or regions that allow, or encourage, overt persecution of my children. No believer is exempt.

His tactics can be blatant or covert, depending on what he thinks will be most effective. His strategy is to try to dishearten, distract, and disempower, so my children will feel weak, weary, and abandoned. He utilizes a "whatever it takes" approach.

Whenever those who love me step onto the front lines, there will be hostile resistance. That should not surprise you. I have warned you about the tenacious nature of tribulation. Just remember I am always greater! You need my protection. My power is infinite. His is not. Ultimately, nothing can separate my children and me.

You are mine. Bring all your needs to me. I will not always give you an exemption from everything he hurls your direction. But I will give you what you need to walk through it gracefully, if you are willing to lean fully on me.

Bring me your envy when you see those prosper who don't belong to me. It is not in our enemy's best interest to oppose them. He wants them to pledge allegiance to anything, but me. Stay close today. My magnificence prevails over every minefield. Depend on my direction, strength, comfort, grace and peace to navigate what is ahead.

I love you,
Abba

POOLS OF BLESSING

"When they walk through the Valley of Weeping, it will become a place of springs where pools of blessing and refreshment collect after rains!" PSALM 84:6

"immersed in tears, yet always filled with deep joy;"
2 CORINTHIANS 6:10

My Child,

Because I will go with you through the painful valleys of your life, my presence can transform your sorrow into something supernatural, beautiful and life-giving. I can cause eternal beauty to blossom from the broken ground of your heart.

If you will let me, I can sow my peace, comfort, love, truth, joy and endurance into those deep fissures of pain. Your tears are not wasted. From the wellspring of your sorrow, I can create refreshing springs and pools of blessing to revive and encourage you and others.

> *"I can cause eternal beauty to blossom from the broken ground of your heart."*

Please allow me to redeem your grief. I am the God of creation and re-creation. I can create something glorious from what is formless and void. But I can also reanimate the ruins of your life to create a stunning display of my splendor.

I love you,
Abba

My Abba,

Once again, this morning you have given me a precious glimpse of your beauty. My circumstances pale in the light of your love. I still hurt, but as the song says, "my afflictions are eclipsed by your glory, when I realize just how beautiful you are and how great your affections are for me." *

I love the imagery of you creating reservoirs of refreshment from my tears. What a redemptive picture! I also find comfort in Paul's comment on the mystery of suffering while experiencing joy in your presence ..."immersed in tears, yet always filled with deep joy;" I can't fully comprehend how I can mourn my circumstances and rejoice in you at the same time. But I know it happens.

I guess you experience sorrow and joy at the same time as you walk with us in this world. All in one moment, some of those you love are suffering atrocities while someone else is giving birth to the beautiful baby for whom she fervently prayed.

(paraphrased excerpt), "How He Loves," David Crowder

Some are brutally persecuted while others reach their greatest pinnacles. Some are perishing while others receive the gift of eternity with you. That is hard to wrap my mind around. But if you experience joy and sadness simultaneously, I feel less troubled by this emotional paradox in which I walk.

I choose to trust you today to engage in profound re-creation in my life. I know one spring rain can cause the desert floor to burst with beauty. Take the arid landscape of my circumstances and create a supernatural oasis where we can drink from your fountain of delights.

I love you,
Mollie

SWIMMING WITH ALLIGATORS

"I know how to live on almost nothing or with everything.
I have learned the secret of living in every situation,
whether it is with a full stomach or empty, with plenty
or little. For I can do everything through Christ,
who gives me strength."
PHILIPPIANS 4:12–13

My Abba,

This week has left me exhausted physically and emotionally. Watching my son suffer has been excruciating. I desperately desire to soothe, rescue, take his place, chase the pain away. But I can't.

I want you to heal him. That is the cry of my heart. Please, Abba. I want the miraculous ending and really don't want you to take your time, if I am being honest.

But even if you don't give me what I want, please whisper to me again "the secret of living in every situation." Although pain has hung around like a tenacious antagonist for much of my story, you have shown me unquenchable life. You have revealed it to me in both the glorious and the gutter moments. I know the secret to living well, in all circumstances, is to live in a vibrant relationship with you, no matter where I am on this road to heaven.

Because you are my supernatural strength, my song and my salvation, I can rejoice in your presence in the midst of all my circumstances. You are my glorious love, hope, and peace. You are my infinite grace, compassion, and forgiveness. Those eternal gifts you give me are beautiful, even when I paddle with you through the painful, alligator-infested, swampy parts of our journey.

Whether my storyline is delightful or desperate, I acknowledge you as the hero and director. Then I can appreciate your presence in the spotlight no matter what else is taking place.

I love you,
Mollie

My Child,

I am sorry you are in pain. I am here. I can carry your sorrow. You have discovered that the sustaining secret of joy amidst any circumstance is in me. But that joy runs thin, if you are consumed by your situation. Look at me. We can do this.

When you are desperate to live in the truth of who I am, you do find all you need in me. In these times, I am not on your checklist of things you should get to but might not, because I am not interesting enough, important enough, or beautiful enough, to hold your attention. My presence is as crucial to you as your next breath.

Don't try to manipulate the hard stuff into something in which you take joy. Taking joy in pain is masochistic. Sometimes you will not find the silver lining, profound reason, or happy ending for the tragedies in your life. But keeping company with me in the midst of the pain-filled chapters will make all the difference.

I am infinitely joyful. So my presence can always be the glorious object of your joy — even when we are swimming with alligators.

I love you,
Abba

LIFE IN THE BRIAR PATCH

"Three different times I begged God to make me well again. Each time he said, 'No. But I am with you; that is all you need. My power shows up best in weak people.' Now I am glad to boast about how weak I am; I am glad to be a living demonstration of Christ's power, instead of showing off my own power and abilities.

"Since I know it is all for Christ's good, I am quite happy about 'the thorn,' and about insults and hardships, persecutions and difficulties; for when I am weak, then I am strong—the less I have, the more I depend on him." 2 CORINTHIANS 12:8–10

My Child,

I know you want answers, but I have some questions for you this morning. Do you really believe I am all you need? What if I don't choose to heal you? What if it glorifies me more for you to minister to others from a place of weakness?

"Does my character change when your life gets difficult and I don't provide a smooth passage to paradise?"

What if my light is more apparent shining through all the broken places in your armor? How will you feel about me if I don't provide

the rescue, remedy your pain, and fix your circumstances? What will you believe about me if the insults, hardships, sickness and difficulties continue?

Do you believe this is evidence that my love has lessened for you? Does my character change when your life gets difficult and I don't provide a smooth passage to paradise?

I love you, my child, with a perfect, changeless, endless love. That does not shift with the rolling landscape of your life. Many times the journey will get tough. The winds of adversity may beat you down, you may stumble over the sharp rocks of betrayal, and get caught in a torrential downpour of hardships.

I will sustain you. My love is better than life — even the most polished, perfect life you can imagine.

I love you,
Abba

My Abba,

When I have my head on straight, I do believe you are all I need. How can you lack any good thing? You are flawless. When I warm my heart by the blaze of your perfect beauty, I get to experience some of that glory. It is breathtaking. The closer I get, the more magnificent you look. The more our intimacy grows, the more I am satisfied.

I guess all of this begs the question, "Am I really committed to your glory or is that just something I say when I feel spiritual?" If I am committed to your glory above all things, then any, and every, situation is just another opportunity for you to create a display of your splendor in my life.

If you don't choose to heal me, I know tomorrow can still be better than today as I move closer to your heart. I want to be a part of this epic adventure with you. Increase my capacity for your love each day. Please heighten my delight in you and my sense of your delight in me. The shadowy "what-ifs" about tomorrow seem to fade as I walk into the glorious light of your love.

Please use every hurt, struggle and victory to accomplish your plans and purposes in, and through, me. I will be one of your broken beauties, if that is what you want. I don't think I will ever be ecstatic about the "thorns," but I will find joy in you in the midst of the briar patch. Today, in my weaknesses, draw me near to your heart so that I might be overwhelmed by your beauty, not by the brambles in my life.

I love you,
Mollie

MAKING MONET

"'You are seeing things merely from a human point of view, not from God's.' Then Jesus said to his disciples, 'If any of you wants to be my follower, you must give up your own way, take up your cross, and follow me. If you try to hang on to your life, you will lose it. But if you give up your life for my sake, you will save it.'"
MATTHEW 16:23b–25

My Abba,

If I limit myself to a "human point of view," much of my life could look painful and pointless. I wanted a life with more rose petals, fewer thorns. That was my ambition. That was my dream.

Images of painters Picasso and Monet are coming to mind. If I am honest, I wanted less in my life that looked like Picasso's blue period and more that looked like Monet. I imagined my "abundant life" would be marked by frequent strolls through chapters that resembled Monet's garden scenes.

But this passage doesn't sound like you promise a rose petal life to any of us. Shouldering my cross and giving up my life for you does not sound like the gospel of healthy, wealthy, and happily-ever-after.

Please show me more today about what you call "true life." I know my idea of life is somewhat stunted by my humanity. I don't want to clutch at a life designed by my limited imagination and lose the true life you perfectly crafted for me.

I choose to release what I cannot keep and receive from you what I cannot lose.

I love you,
Mollie

My Child,

From your "human point of view," you can often feel hopeless and trapped. You know when you use your camera how important the right lens is. You can completely miss capturing the essential moment without it.

True life is like that. If you ask for my lens, I can show you what is eternal, vital, and beautiful. It will not always involve pastel, sun-dappled flowers, but the ways I redeem it are perfectly magnificent.

You are still holding on to certain outcomes as key to true life. But they are useless to give you life. I am the Author of life. I will give you the power to "take up your cross and follow me."

I never ask you to just try harder. I only ask you to rely on me for everything you need to walk well. Ask for and receive my provision for you. That is what makes my burden light. Not the denial of your cross, but the reality of my provision and power offered freely to those who follow me.

In reality, there were snakes, ants, mosquitoes, and bees in the gardens Monet painted. Sometimes it was too hot. Other times it was too cold. But beauty triumphed!

Let me lighten your burden today. I will give you the grace for true life in your garden.

I love you,
Abba

WAS IT BECAUSE...

"As Jesus was walking along, he saw a man who had been blind from birth. 'Rabbi,' his disciples asked him, 'Why was this man born blind? Was it because of his own sins or his parents' sins?' 'It was not because of his sins or his parents' sins,' Jesus answered. 'This happened so the power of God could be seen in him.'"
JOHN 9:1–3

My Abba,

I can't imagine the challenges of being born blind at the time this man lived. In addition to the obvious struggles directly created by his disability, he and his family were plagued by stigma and blame. In their culture, the common beliefs about suffering seemed to fuel accusations and conjecture as to whose sin caused this man's disability. Insult added to injury.

I am so weary of suffering. Not just my suffering, but that of countless others. I find the plight of children being hurt by people they should be able to trust especially tragic. My heart breaks for the persecuted church. I grieve as disease, famine, and injustice scour the planet.

I want your love to invade all this darkness and obliterate the pain. We are desperate for relief.

It doesn't help me personally cope when people ask me questions like, "Do you really think you can glorify God, if he doesn't heal you?" Then there is the cacophony of voices that have offered comments like, "If you just had more faith, God would remove your pain, heal your disease, fix your circumstances, order your world, and do away with the stubborn stains in your messy life." I know these clueless "comforters" sometimes mean well, but they leave my heart feeling trampled by their runaway, errant advice.

It's not like I have the answers. But you know I have stopped asking the "Was it because?" question. I just know after decades of chewing on this topic, I will not be satisfied with the meager explanations we try to paste like tiny band aids on the wounds from which we hemorrhage.

You allow suffering. A lot of it. And most of the time, I don't get it.

But I will not forsake relationship with you, even, in the absence of answers. I am not willing to let the unexplained pain rob me of your glorious presence. I will not bite the hand that feeds me. Why would I distance myself from the only One who sustains and nourishes me?

This passage gives me fresh hope to pray for your power to be revealed to people in the midst of their suffering. Please show yourself in compelling ways. Draw them (and me) to the reality of your love forever. Let your power be seen in us.

I love you,
Mollie

My Child,

I want you to see more clearly what I have for you. I want that sight I give you to bring me glory. I want my demonstration of power in your life to point to my perfection. I want others to see how glorious I am.

I know over the years as you have suffered, some people have questioned your faith and devotion to me. I have not allowed your suffering because you are not doing it right. There is not some buried sin I am trying to uproot. You would not be a better display of my splendor if you enjoyed perfect health, wealth, and all the cookies in the cookie jar.

I know most days you are tired and want to come home. There will be a time for that. You are time-bound and the clock can seem savagely slow.

Today, I give you my strength and courage to press on. Though sometimes you feel shattered, my power and love are streaming across the jagged edges of your heart creating a kaleidoscope for my light.

Although I am not in the habit of explaining all my reasons to you for allowing suffering, I promise to constantly redeem the pain of this world with my light and love.

I love you,
Abba

DEFY THE DARKNESS

"We sent him to strengthen you, to encourage you in your faith, and to keep you from being shaken by the troubles you were going through. But you know that we are destined for such troubles. Even while we were with you, we warned you that troubles would soon come — and they did, as you well know."

"How can we thank God enough for you because of all the joy that comes only from our God?" 1 THESSALONIANS 3:2b–4, 9

My Abba,

Thank you so much for this truth. Again today, I need it. Sometimes, I am still surprised by times of trouble. Despite the persistent show-and-tell to the contrary, I can slide into thinking I am not "destined for such troubles." My wishful thinking coaxes me to believe I should get to live a comfortable, gentle life. If problems do roll in, they should always be properly chaperoned by a speedy and complete solution.

The dilemma is that my trials are no longer wrapped in the pretty, Pollyanna package of denial. I have become intimately acquainted with the downpour of difficulties in my life. And in passages like this, I witness the guarantee of troubles. So why am I surprised when life gets hard?

I guess I buy into the endless messages from my culture. It chirps that I just need to slip into something new — that heaven on earth will come with the next purchase, achievement, relationship or change in circumstances. These are the gods of our day.

*"Make my love for you grow ...
like a well-watered garden
that is resilient and thrives
even under a blazing sun."*

Thank you for reminding me today that even in the midst of troubles, you are real, present, and can give me your joy. Please, make my love for you grow healthier and heartier, like a well-watered garden that is resilient and thrives even under a blazing sun.

While I sit here with you, I am confident that the lesser things never hold a candle to the unspeakable gifts I find in you. And then my day happens, and I can get lost in the weeds. Come what may, troubles and all, please help me remain grounded in the reality of your love and joy today.

I love you,
Mollie

My Child,

Our enemy's most profound deception is the mirage of satisfaction in which he wraps his counterfeits. Despite his sloppy sales pitch, sometimes you buy it.

Rely on me to give you eyes to see the fraud. I offer the freedom and privilege of living in truth. All joy, peace, grace and love is found in me. Only I can give you these treasures — even in the midst of troubles.

When you choose to walk with me, you can see the magnificence of my gifts that defy the darkness of unmentionable evil. Gifts, which glisten gloriously like fresh, untamed water making music under a voracious desert sun. Gifts, which refuse to perish in the blazing mouth of an angry fire. Gifts, which stand grounded and immovable, even in a savage torrent.

I love you,
Abba

CRACKED CLAY

"For God, who said, 'Light shall shine out of darkness,' is the One who has shone in our hearts to give the light of the knowledge of the glory of God in the face of Christ. But we have this treasure in earthen containers, so that the extraordinary greatness of the power will be of God and not from ourselves; we are afflicted in every way, but not crushed; perplexed, but not despairing; persecuted, but not abandoned; struck down, but not destroyed."
2 CORINTHIANS 4:6–9

My Child,

I am the God who spoke to the dark void of the universe and caused the boundless light of billions of galaxies to burst forth. It should not surprise you that I can illuminate the darkest corners of your heart with the light of the knowledge of my glory. I will never leave you alone in the dark.

If you rest in the priceless provision of my Spirit, you will not lose heart. Lay down all that is not of me, so that I may reveal my glory through you. I have entrusted the treasure of my Spirit to your earthen vessel. I can demonstrate my surpassing greatness through you. I am able to use all those battle cracks as portals for my radiance. This allows everyone to see my power does not originate with you.

> *"I am able to use all those battle cracks as portals for my radiance."*

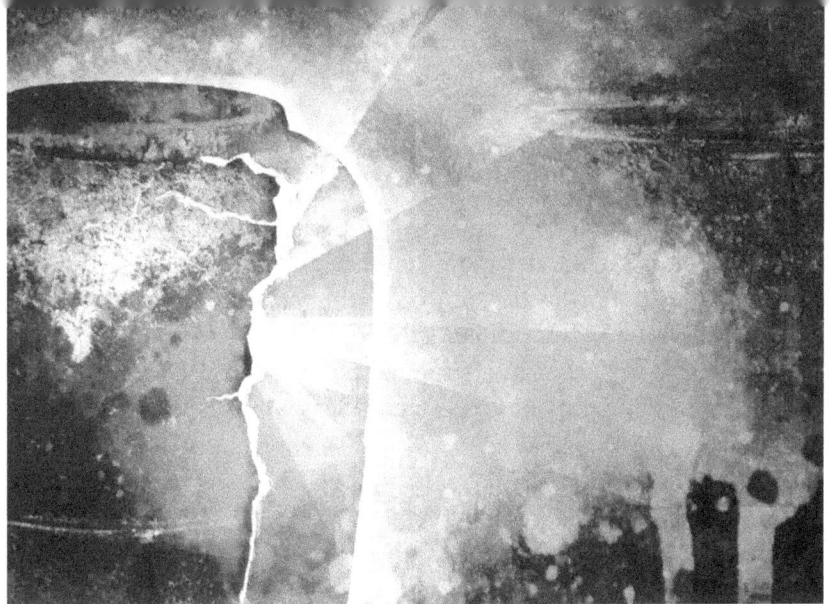

You have been afflicted in many ways, but not crushed. You have been perplexed, but did not despair. You have been persecuted, but not abandoned. You have been struck down, but not destroyed. Christ's death and life have been reflected in you. This brings me glory.

So do not lose heart. Only your flesh is fading. Your spirit (which is eternal) continues to blossom as you thrive in my presence. Trust me. All your struggles can give birth to an eternal glory that is beyond anything you can imagine.

I love you,
Abba

My Abba,

Sometimes I want to hide my cracks and chips, so I look smoother — more unblemished to others. Please help me to resist the urge to cover up and play picture-perfect. We both know that is not reality.

When I receive the eternal beauty you have to offer, my heart is ecstatic. Immersed in your grace, love and truth, I realize I am gloriously privileged and satisfied. I want to be a finely tuned instrument for your influence. I want your power to be evident in me — your glory pouring through every broken place in my life.

Thank you that you have sustained me, especially in affliction. You have kept me from being crushed, despairing, and destroyed. You have never abandoned me.

As the years pass and my earth suit grows weaker, I look forward to all the ways you are igniting my spirit with the spark of your love. Each day, please make me more sensitive to your leading. I want to recognize the opportunities you offer this cracked clay pot to be a luminous vessel for your brilliance.

Thank you for being my perpetual power source. I want to shine for you in a way that makes it perfectly clear who has the power.

I love you,
Mollie

IN THIS LABYRINTH

What do I do with this wilted faith?

SEEING THROUGH DOUBT

"Then Jesus told him, 'You believe because you have seen me. Blessed are those who believe without seeing me.' The disciples saw Jesus do many other miraculous signs in addition to the ones recorded in this book. But these are written so that you may continue to believe that Jesus is the Messiah, the Son of God, and that by believing in him you will have life by the power of his name." JOHN 20:29–31

My Child,

I have blessed you with the gift of belief, even though you have not yet seen me face to face. When you receive this spectacular blessing, my generosity permeates your heart.

 I can then offer you what you need to release that persistent covey of questions demanding explanations for life's pain. Sometimes doubt will slip in through the door uninvited and begin splashing graffiti on the walls of your mind. That is to be expected. Your finite mind cannot pin down and sort out my infinite reasoning. Bring doubt to me. I can help you show it to the exit.

 I have given you trust that I am God. When you allow me to draw you into the glorious respite of my love, you experience me as your One-and-Only. This nourishes your confidence that I am perfectly strong, trustworthy, able and reliable, even though you don't see me with your eyes or understand all I am doing. When you put your trust in me, you thrive.

 Spend time with me in my Word. Life-changing, supernatural truth is written there about you, others and me, so you may thrive in your relationships. As your trust in me grows, you will have an increasingly richer life by the power of my name.

GENEROSITY: *readiness to give more than is expected or necessary*

Your vigor, enthusiasm, and vitality in me will flourish. That is the vibrant life I intend for you.

I love you,
Abba

My Abba,

I need this truth. We both know I am not a spotless woman of faith. Doubt splatter-paints my soul at times. Nothing about that is artistic.

But more and more, as I spend my days with you, I cannot deny your stunning presence. You are endlessly beautiful and your love for me is irresistible. Your generous supernatural gifts lead me into a more joyful connection with you.

> *"Doubt splatter-paints my soul at times. Nothing about that is artistic."*

Thank you for the ways you enliven me with your truth. You give me the power not to quit, even when the turbulence of life makes me desperately desire heaven. Please give me the trust and grace I need to thrive in the midst of whatever comes to pass today — and tomorrow.

I love you,
Mollie

CAPTIVATED

"At this point many of his disciples turned away and deserted him. Then Jesus turned to the Twelve and asked, 'Are you also going to leave?' Simon Peter replied, 'Lord, to whom would we go? You have the words that give eternal life. We believe, and we know you are the Holy One of God.'" JOHN 6:66–69

My Abba,

I would like to believe I always stand in the confidence Peter expresses in this passage. I would like to think I am always faithful to the truth that you are the only Source of life.

I would like to rest assured I will never go to anything or anyone else seeking to find that which you alone can give me. I would like to believe doubt won't ever show its disturbing face on my doorstep.

But I want to live in reality. And reality paints a much less glowing picture of my life with you. Just like Peter, I make strong, convincing confessions of my love for you. And like Peter, I mean it. But also like Peter, I sometimes entertain lies about you and act accordingly.

Even though I have never made an audible, public confession denying you, my choices, actions and attitudes expose my heart. My feet can be staunchly faithful to your path one day and run renegade the next.

Please give me the rock-solid confidence and love for you that always cries out, "Lord, to whom would I go? You have the words that give eternal life. I know you are the Holy One of God."

I love you,
Mollie

My Child,

How many times have the following thoughts covertly crossed your mind? "If you chase these things, they will satisfy you more than what God has for you. You are missing out."

Here is the untainted truth: Every time you make a choice to clutch at something other than my matchless plans for your life, you are grabbing a fist full of sand. It may feel momentarily warm and interesting in your hand, but it is not lasting and life-giving. Imagine it rushing to the ground through your fingers.

These inferior things will attempt to sell you a dream, but when you wake, you will be left trying to rid yourself of the disappointing, gritty residue of misplaced expectations.

Intellectually, you know it is impossible to be more satisfied with a life filled with what is inferior and ultimately less satisfying. Empowered by my love, I offer you an opportunity to participate in what is eternally significant and meaningful. I want you to thrive. I can't help myself. That is who I am.

Let me cleanse your eyes from the smoke that obscures your view of me today. I want to wipe away the soot of your sin, so you can see me more clearly. My beauty is irresistible. If you catch a glimpse, you will be captivated.

I love you,
Abba

IN THE LABYRINTH

"Show me the right path, O Lord. Point out the right road
for me to follow. Lead me by your truth and teach me,
for you are the God who saves me. All day long
I put my hope in you."
PSALM 25: 4–5

My Abba,

Please illuminate your path for me this morning. I feel a little lost in this shifting labyrinth. As some of the quarantine restrictions are lifted, I want to make wise choices. Left on my own, I cannot navigate all these twists and turns effectively. What are wise practices? I don't want to live in fear, but I want to choose responsible strategies that seem prudent for others and myself.

You are the only one who knows the whole truth about our current crisis. Even the experts seem to have opinions that are prone to morph as quickly as the shapes of clouds on a windy day. It is difficult to sort fact from fiction as the frenzied wild cards of prediction fly across the table.

I need you to guide my mind, body and spirit. I am no match for what lurks in these unknown passages. I need you to tell me the truth you want me to know about you, me, and this confusing maze. Sometimes I feel I am being overly cautious. Sometimes I think I am not being careful enough.

Please give me clarity by the power of your Spirit. Nourish my hope in you all day long. Please grow my confident expectation in you and give me everything I need to stay on the right road with you.

I love you,
Mollie

LABYRINTH: *a complicated irregular network of passages or paths in which it is difficult to find one's way*

My Child,

I am the God who saves you. It may not be the rescue you have in mind, but my plans for you are flawless. I will lead you by my truth.

I have liberated you from a hopeless life without me. Because of our forever connection, I am continually protecting you from your shortsighted impulses and misplaced plans.

Don't settle for the sandcastle schemes you can create on your own. I have the benefit of a perfect, eternal perspective. I can see forever. It is all "now" to me. I AM here and up ahead. I am here with you now, preparing you for then. And I am there in the "then," preparing it for you.

> *"I am infinitely more radiant than the sun and all the stars in the universe combined."*

I know the signposts may seem obscured in these tangled times, but I am with you. And I am not a flashlight god you put batteries in and hold in your hand. I am infinitely more radiant than the sun and all the stars in the universe combined. Put your hope in me. Let me light your way.

I love you,
Abba

YOUR ROAD, REALITY, AND ROOTS

"Jesus said to him, 'I am the way, and the truth, and the life; no one comes to the Father except through Me.'" JOHN 14:6

My Child,

Run to me as a delighted child who is completely confident in the love of your Father. Approach me unabashedly, reveling in my unending devotion for you. My arms are open wide. Because of your trust in Christ, you have unfettered access, a clear path, to my throne room. He alone makes that possible.

The words of Christ recorded in this passage are my words, also. I am your reality—the only truth on which you can fully depend. I am your vitality — the power essential to your wellbeing and healthy growth. I am your road, your reality and your roots.

> *"Run to me as a delighted child who is completely confident in the love of your Father."*

You can follow this path I have for you into what is real and good, nourished by all that I have to help you thrive. Well-planted, well-watered, well-fed, growing toward the light.

I will show you where to walk, guard you from deception, and empower you to make the journey. I will call to you daily, "This is the road I want you to walk. This is why you need to stay on it. Here is my power to enable you to do so."

WAY: path for traveling, access, entrance   TRUTH: reality, fact
LIFE: vitality, vigor, energy; the power required for well-being and healthy growth

I want to make this journey with you. You will find imperishable joy in me, even in the most difficult parts of the path. I can make you sure-footed when the earth feels as though it may crumble beneath your feet.

I love you,
Abba

My Abba,

Thank you for your devoted embrace this morning. Your unconditional acceptance draws me in.

You faithfully show me reality. But I still have the capacity to entertain delusion. I can choose poorly minutes after basking in your truth and beauty. My sin nature is persistent and convincing.

I thrive in the shadow of your wings. But our enemy never gives up. No matter how perfectly convincing you are, I can, somehow, still wander off again into the mirage. Please continue to draw me back onto the life-giving path you have for me. Keep nourishing me with reality. I need your constant truth about what is best for me.

And please, perpetually remind me that you are offering all the power required to thrive on this journey. I want to be caught up in your adventure, walking the path you have chosen for me, blinders cast aside, and well fed by your Spirit.

I love you,
Mollie

OVERFLOWING HOPE

"I pray that God, the source of hope, will fill you completely with joy and peace because you trust in him. Then you will overflow with confident hope through the power of the Holy Spirit." ROMANS 15:13

My Child,

I am the God of hope. As you place your hope in me, I will fill you with peace and joy. The hope I give is supernatural, imperishable, and empowered by my Spirit.

Your days now are filled with uncertainty and grief at the ways this epidemic is stealing life as you know it. Put your hope in me. I am the only one who can bring beauty from ashes, joy instead of mourning, and a garment of praise instead of a spirit of despair.

Put your hope in the certainty that I will provide you with every spiritual blessing as you thrive in my presence. I will sustain you with my grace gifts — my love, peace, goodness and joy. My beauty, strength, endurance and faithfulness. My power, mercy, wisdom and compassion.

My provision is flawless and endless. Saturate your heart and mind with the truth of who I am. That will build your hope in me, even if, everything around you collapses.

I love you,
Abba

My Abba,

Thank you for nourishing me with your truth. I don't do anything well when I am famished. Please feed me this morning so that I can face the day well nourished by your Spirit.

HOPE: A feeling of expectation and desire for a certain thing to happen; A person or thing that may help or save someone

These definitions of hope really challenge me to think about in what, or in whom, I put my hope. Am I inspired to endure by my hope in you? Or, do I simply have a "desire for a certain thing to happen?" Am I putting my hope in you or in a certain outcome?

Honestly, I think my answer is both. There are definitely things I hope will happen. I hope this relentless plague will be defeated soon. I hope you will ease this suffering that is wounding our world. In the fierce wake of tragedy, I hope those affected will be restored spiritually, emotionally and physically.

With that said, good outcomes are not my God. You are my God. Great circumstances are not my Savior. You are my Savior. I hope for good things to happen. But I refuse to worship those good things.

Worshiping anyone or anything other than you is eventually followed by the sound of my idols smashing against the rocks of my misplaced expectations.

I want to experience your love more deeply. I want to place my hope in you and what is paramount to you.

When I choose you and life is still hard, I can draw a deeper breath of your glorious presence and live. I never feel more alive than in those moments — living in your love, comforted and carried by your eternal, infinite provision.

As you walk with me through this season, your love is building new beauty in my bruised heart. Thank you for creating in my life another supernatural monument to your glory.

I love you,
Mollie

HONEYSUCKLE ON THE WIND

"God showed how much he loved us by sending his one and only Son into the world so that we might have eternal life through him. This is real love—not that we loved God, but that he loved us and sent his Son as a sacrifice to take away our sins. Dear friends, since God loved us that much, we surely ought to love each other. No one has ever seen God. But if we love each other, God lives in us, and his love is brought to full expression in us."
1 JOHN 4:9–12

My Child,

There is not a way for you to fully grasp the joy of our endless communion in the Trinity. Before Christ came to earth, the Spirit, Son and I enjoyed an indescribable, uninterrupted glorious intimacy. While Christ was on earth, there was a temporary, sacrificial interruption of that perfect communion. But our love for mankind compelled us to make that choice.

It was the only way in our perfect economy of justice that my holy math would work. I provided what was needed to satisfy the part of the equation only I could satisfy. I needed a perfect substitution. Your sin plus my holy payment for your sin is the only combination of two variables that results in you spending forever with me.

But that required my Son to leave the flawless symphony of the Trinity for a season. You should never take that for granted. Your freedom came at a high price. Not just your once-and-for-all freedom, but your daily freedom. When you are entertaining a certain sin, remem-

ber you have the choice to rely on my power to resist that path because of my sacrifice for your escape.

I love you infinitely and I want you to walk in that love. I live in you and want to express my love through you. You do not find some people in your life very lovable. That is where my miraculous power truly shines. I will love them through you.

Open your heart for my infinite, unconditional, perfect love to flow, not only to you, but through you.

I love you,
Abba

My Abba,

Thank you for your perfect love. I realize I have only a slight hint of the magnificent reality of your embrace. I think the way I now experience your love is something like catching the faint fragrance of honeysuckle on the wind as a child, when I walked near the fence that wore it like an ivory spring shawl. Distinct and delicious, but nothing like burying my face in the blossoms.

One day, when you welcome me home, I will bury my face in your beauty. But thank you that even in this life, I am more and more keenly aware of your exquisite fragrance as we walk together. What a bright future I have when I consider the possibility of an increasingly deeper experience of your love, grace, truth, kindness, joy, beauty and all of your other dazzling qualities!

I want to walk as a child defined by your matchless grace. I want my life to be a visible expression of your love. Thank you that you give me the power to shed my natural tendencies and baggage and reach for you, instead. Please make those choices glaringly clear to me. I want to walk so closely by your side that the perfume of your presence wears off on me.

I love you,
Mollie

ONE OF THOSE

"For I testify about them that they have a zeal for God, but not in accordance with knowledge. For not knowing about God's righteousness and seeking to establish their own, they did not subject themselves to the righteousness of God. For Christ is the end of the Law for righteousness to everyone who believes."

"if you confess with your mouth Jesus as Lord, and believe in your heart that God raised Him from the dead, you will be saved; for with the heart a person believes, resulting in righteousness, and with the mouth he confesses, resulting in salvation. For the Scripture says, 'Whoever believes in Him will not be put to shame.'"

"'I was found by those who did not seek Me,
I revealed Myself to those who did not ask for Me.'"
ROMANS 10:2–4, 9–11, 20

My Child,

I am glad for your zeal. But I want your zeal to always be steeped in reality — true knowledge of me.

Many in your culture believe they should have the freedom to shape me into a god fashioned by their own tastes. Someone in keeping with current whims. Someone politically correct, ground down by the tides of your times.

To them, I am so last century. My ways are clearly not their ways. And my thoughts are definitely not their thoughts.

Don't be tempted to use a filter on my features when some might not find them attractive. An authentic relationship with me won't flourish in the soil of self-deception.

Proclaim the good news about who I am, unabashedly, all the days of your life. My truth is going out to the ends of the earth and you can be a part of that.

I revealed myself to you, even though you were not seeking me. There are others just like you. I am reaching out to wayward, stubborn ones. Come with me as I reveal myself to them. Some will accept my offer and their transformation will be stunning. You won't want to miss this.

I love you,
Abba

My Abba,

Thank you for giving me a growing passion for you. I want to experience you more deeply each day as you fuel my desire to live for your glory.

Thank you for reminding me that my forever connection with you is made possible by Christ's righteousness, not mine. Thank you for your fierce faithfulness to me. Because your provision is faultless, I will never have to march in the shame parade again.

I would ask that you equip me with everything I need on a daily basis to proclaim your good news to those who might not have the slightest notion they need you. Thank you for revealing yourself to me, even though I wasn't seeking you. I had no clue you wanted a relationship with me.

Then, you opened my eyes. And there you were! Utterly magnificent, yet deeply concerned for me! Spectacularly powerful, yet tender! Perfectly just, yet absolutely merciful!

> *"I had no clue you wanted a relationship with me."*

Don't let me write off the ones who look self-sufficient and disinterested in you. I was one of those. Don't let me overlook the self-confident, successful, seemingly put-together ones. I was one of those. Don't let me ignore the busy ones who don't seem to have time for you. I was one of those.

Give me your heart for everyone who crosses my path. Please pour out your love through me today!

I love you,
Mollie

RABBIT HOLES AND REALITY

What does truth look like?

DRY UP, BLOW UP, OR GROW UP

"But the time is coming—indeed it's here now—when true worshipers will worship the Father in spirit and in truth. The Father is looking for those who will worship him that way. For God is Spirit, so those who worship him must worship in spirit and in truth." JOHN 4:23–24

My Abba,

I want to be a true worshiper. Please show me how to more fully express my reverence and adoration for you today.

To me, worshiping in spirit and truth seems wild and grounded. Ethereal and tethered to truth. Mysterious and factual. Engaging emotions and mind. Supernatural but based in reality. Meditating on what is glorious but real. The healthy marriage of heart and mind. The real me connecting with the real you.

I know I can worship you (express my reverence and adoration for you) through serving, loving others, yielding to your will, writing, teaching, and countless other ways. Everything can become an act of worship when I am empowered by your Spirit, seeking to glorify you. But it seems when I worship you through music, the non-physical part of me is more fully engaged.

My emotions, my soul, my true self, the eternal me is drawn into your presence. You leave me breathless, joyfully overwhelmed. More

---

SPIRIT: the nonphysical part of a person that is the seat of emotions and character, the soul, the part of a person regarded as a person's true self, capable of surviving physical death or separation
WORSHIP: the feeling or expression of reverence and adoration

permeable to your truth. Less earthbound. So, for me, music that draws my heart to you is a crucial part of my worship.

I remember what a friend once said, "If you only worship in truth, you're going to dry up. If you only worship in spirit, you're going to blow up. But if you worship in spirit and truth, you're going to grow up."

I want to grow up. Please deepen my experience of your presence today. I want to worship you in spirit and truth.

I love you,
Mollie

My Child,

You have seen many forms of worship. Some of my children worship the Father, Son and Holy Scriptures. I don't want you to worship truth. I want my truth to strengthen your desire to worship me.

In other settings, you have seen how worshiping in spirit alone, without an anchor set steadfastly in the truth, allows an undercurrent of fallacy to carry people out to sea.

If you don't embrace the truth about a person and just "love" the façade of another, you do not truly love that person. This is akin to "loving" a fictitious character in a book or film. Infatuation with an engaging fantasy is not true love and cannot be a basis for authentic worship.

> *"To be lover and beloved*
> *is to truly know*
> *and be known."*

 A love relationship needs a healthy dose of reality. To be lover and beloved is to truly know and be known. The more you know me, the more your love for me will grow. Our bond will not flourish without emotions. But the emotions have to be based on what is real.

 I don't want you to admire me from a distance. When we engage at a heart level, you don't just respect me from across the room. I designed you for a relationship with me that runs deeper than an intellectual assent to my deity, character and power.

 I want intimate, genuine connection with you. Don't try to dress yourself up for me. I am not interested in the masquerade. I love the way I made you. I want to connect with the beloved one I created, not some pretense fueled by the person you think you should be.

 Ask the Holy Spirit to engage your spirit and mind in true adoration. In the Trinity, we endlessly celebrate each other. We want to draw you into that celebration.

I love you,
Abba

TREASURE TROVE

"You made me; you created me. Now give me the sense to follow your commands."

"Look upon me with love; teach me your decrees."

"Your laws are perfect and completely trustworthy."

"Your laws are always right; help me to understand them so I may live."

"I rejoice in your word like one who discovers a great treasure."
PSALM 119: 73, 135, 138, 144, 162

My Abba,

For a season, I approached time in your Word like I regarded time spent eating a healthy salad. Nutritious and necessary for my wellbeing but requiring a lot of discipline for daily consumption. I did not savor it as I swallowed.

I realize discipline is good. But I want the extraordinary way you communicate with us through your Word to spawn something more in me than a desire to check some spiritual duty off my must-do list.

If you, the Most High God who spoke the galaxies into being, desire to communicate with me, I want to stand in awe of that indescribable privilege.

I want to experience, like the psalmist, everything you designed your Word to do. Thank you that Scripture is living and active. When empowered by your Spirit, you assure me your words will never perch listlessly on the page.

Thank you for revitalizing my passion for your Word. I have thought about the "whys." The only new practice is the simple prayer you have been encouraging me to speak to you before I begin.

You have granted my request to not just let me read the words, but to supernaturally receive your truth in a way that transforms my heart and mind. My time with you has new promise, vigor and delight. I am hungry and expectant.

Although the binding is separating from the pages from years of use, I find myself smiling as I gently flip open the well-worn, curling pages of my Bible. Why? Because I have learned by experience you can breathe power and life into the words and miraculously open the eyes of my heart, if I am willing to ask and receive from you.

> *"My time with you has new promise, vigor and delight. I am hungry and expectant."*

Thank you for gloriously animating the inanimate words inked on the page. The beauty of your truth bursts open within me creating new life. Please continue to sing your fervent love song in my heart.

I love you,
Mollie

My Child,

Scripture gives you my blueprints for life, offering vibrant light, wisdom and direction. My truth can keep you from lying to yourself and settling for the lesser things. I can use it to revive and comfort you, bring you joy and freedom, encourage and restore you.

My principles are no longer popular. The only absolute in your culture is that there are no absolutes.

But in reality, it is right and good for the Creator to impart best practices and principles for his creation. When each created one does what is right in his or her own sight, the results land somewhere between less-than-best and disastrous. You see the evidence of this all around you.

Since I created you, I am intimately acquainted with what is best for you. Don't be fooled by winsome arguments that propel you into the latest thinking of the crowd. Those ideas are fickle — here today and gone tomorrow. There is a way that seems right to people, but only I have an infinite, perfect perspective.

My relentless love compels me to reach out to you with truth. My guidelines for an abundant life will not always make sense to you. Trust me anyway. I know all things and cannot lie.

I want to awaken your heart each day to the wonder of walking with me. Look to my Word for trustworthy, true signposts pointing you to my gracious path of life.

I love you,
Abba

RABBIT HOLES AND REALITY

"Lead me by your truth and teach me, for you are the God who saves me. All day long I put my hope in you." PSALM 25:5

My Child,

Don't drift along numbly taking my gifts for granted. My truth is another one of my magnificent gifts. It points out who I am and my matchless aspirations for you and others. Don't settle for less.

No matter how convincing and sensational the world's imaginations look, I am the God of reality. I cannot shore up the fallacious eggshell castles crafted by human hands. Stay aware and grounded in my truth.

Believe it. Breathe it in. Live it out. I am advocating for the truth to triumph in you. I cannot possibly desire anything else.

When my truth points to your frailties, don't despise my correction. Your weakness is fertile ground for me to show my power. No matter how often you are weak, I remain perpetually, infinitely strong. If you are willing, I will empower you by my Spirit. I will use my truth to cause you to flourish.

Rejoice in that transformation. I am always working to make you more like me. I created you to walk in harmony with my plans and purposes. Stay out of the rabbit holes of popular illusions.

Allow me to immerse you in my extravagant love and life-giving truth. This is an adventure you will never regret.

I love you,
Abba

TRUTH: *that which is in accordance with facts or reality*

My Abba,

Thank you for the ways you have touched my heart with your truth this morning. Please forgive me for the times I allow life to carry me mindlessly downstream.

Wake me up. I want to live enthralled by you and your truth — with an eternal perspective that comes from staying connected with you.

I want to embrace the truth about who you are and who I am to you. I want to embrace the truth about what you have done, what you are doing, and what you will do. I want to embrace your life-giving promises, desires, and purposes.

As I meditate on your truth, please give me the ability to quickly recognize when my thoughts and actions do not align with your heart. I want to sprint to you with my straying heart. When I pretend like there is not an issue, I twist myself into all kinds of disconcerting knots.

I need you to tell me the truth about my shortcomings. Give me the courage and humility to recognize them. Then I would ask you to enter into those weak places and be my glorious Deliverer.

Please make my foremost strength my dependence on you. I want to experience you and your truth in a deeper way today. You are my one true hope "all day long."

I love you,
Mollie

IDENTITY TRUTH

"Lord, my heart is not proud; my eyes are not haughty. I don't concern myself with matters too great or too awesome for me to grasp." PSALM 131:1 (a psalm of David)

My Abba,

If King David truly was not proud or haughty when he wrote this psalm, I find that impressive. For a human, he wielded a lot of power. I have seen power give people a very false sense of their own importance.

At least in one season of his life, I think David considered himself superior, entitled to take whatever he wanted when he wanted it. He took Bathsheba for his pleasure, and then took her husband's life to solidify his ailing cover up. David showed disdain — treating them as unworthy of consideration or respect.

It seems to me that David was seduced by the illusion of his grandeur and bought the superiority lie. He believed, "When I like what I see, it should belong to me." This allowed him to lap up his desire du jour, even if he was stealing from the plates of others. David demonstrated a relentless appetite despite his full belly.

I admit my partial inclination to write him off as a haughty, lying adulterer and murderer. Please forgive me. (I am glad you are more merciful than I am and don't define me by my sin.)

I need to acknowledge some facts. David rose from his humble beginnings as a shepherd to run a country. He was required to make swift, monumental decisions affecting countless people faster than I can choose dinner off the menu at my favorite restaurant. That kind of authority can chase wise thinking into the swamp where honorable intentions drown in the muck.

Maybe David wrote this psalm after you had taught him a thing or two about humility. At some point, he gained a more accurate view

---

PROUD: *having or showing an excessively high opinion of oneself or one's importance*   HAUGHTY: *arrogantly superior and disdainful*   DISDAIN: *the feeling that someone is unworthy of one's consideration or respect*

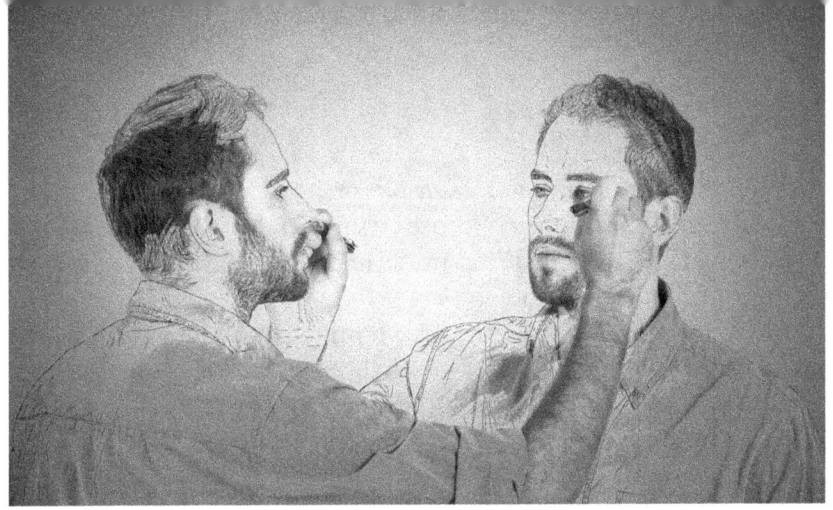

of himself. No matter what he accomplished or how many people fluffed his ego, this sounds like he ultimately grasped reality. He was still just a flesh-and-bones man while you were the One taking care of the "too great and too awesome" matters of the universe. David appears to recognize he couldn't tame his small corner of the world without you. The slightest real brush with you can do that.

Please speak truth to my heart and give me an increasingly more accurate view of who I am and who you are. I don't want to coddle the errant thoughts that flit, at times, around my heart. I don't want to think of myself as inferior or superior. Let me see myself more the way you see me.

I love you,
Mollie

My Child,

Despite the immense earthly authority I gave David, he learned I was still in charge. When he abused his power, I called him out. I didn't let him walk away consequence-free, but his sin was not the end of the story. He repented. I forgave him and brought great redemption in his life.

"You are meticulously crafted.
A uniquely beautiful expression
of my imagination."

David's story is another example of how I can supernaturally transform the human heart. Those changes in David were thorough and dramatic. He laid down pride and haughtiness. He learned whom I created him to be.

Don't try to wear my crown. It is infinitely too heavy for you. Let go of your pride. It wails that you know better than I do what you should do with your life. That is clearly not the truth.

When your pride melts away, it makes room for a life filled with my gifts and your gratitude. I want you to see every breath, day, talent, strength, and opportunity as a gift from me with the beautiful potential to reflect my glory.

You are valuable because I made you in my image. Hold onto the truth of who you are. That "identity truth" will heighten your view of your worth to me. No need for the fallacious mantra of pride. You are not "greater than" or "less than" others. You are meticulously crafted. A uniquely beautiful expression of my imagination.

I love you,
Abba

WISDOM FROM ABOVE

"But the wisdom from above is, first of all, pure. It is also peace loving, gentle at all times, and willing to yield to others. It is full of mercy and the fruit of good deeds. It shows no favoritism and is always sincere." JAMES 3:17

My Abba,

Thank you for giving me some new clarity about wisdom as I spent time with family at my parents' ranch last weekend. My 89-year-old father demonstrated something beyond knowledge. He clearly displayed soundness of action that only comes from experience, knowledge, and good judgment.

It all began when we witnessed my precious, horse-obsessed, four-year-old niece plummet off the back of a large horse. Her untrusty steed relieved Tali of her coveted seat on the saddle and ran off into the woods. My niece's long blonde hair flew every which way, and her bright blue eyes grew as big as saucers. Although our family was left breathless, her injuries only involved a few scrapes. My niece's only concern as she wailed to her dad and mom was, "But can I have another ride?"

Enter Paw Paw — as the grandkids call him. Before he was willing to set her up on another horse, he decided to make sure the next one was feeling obedient. My dad does not have academic knowledge of horses learned through books. He has been riding, breaking, raising or training horses for most of his 89 years.

So with some help from a ranch hand, Dad mounted the horse that might be the next possible candidate. He rode the horse briskly through a pen in patterns around barrels. He backed the horse, ran and walked the horse, and made certain the horse responded reliably to commands.

WISDOM: the soundness of an action or decision with regard to the application of experience, knowledge, and good judgment

When my dad felt the horse was calm and dependable, my niece's parents allowed my dad to lead the horse around the pen with their delighted child back in the saddle. Why? They trusted my dad's wisdom about horses.

They trusted his sound decision-making and follow-through that comes from the "application of experience, knowledge, and good judgment." With horses, Dad's wisdom has been proven in the trenches. I know at my dad's wisest moment, his human wisdom is not perfect, like yours. But it gave me a glimpse of your wisdom, and what the wisdom you give us looks like.

Thank you for introducing yourself to me and offering your supernatural wisdom. Thank you that the gift of your wisdom is pure, brimming with peace, and never harsh. Thank you that your wisdom only produces what is good and encourages us to yield to others when that is constructive. Thank you that your wisdom is merciful, never plays favorites, or flickers hypocritically.

Out of your flawless goodness, please show me your wise plans, and empower me to accomplish what you desire.

I love you,
Mollie

My Child,

I don't give you knowledge about who I am and what I want, so you can hide in an ivory tower of higher consciousness and think deep thoughts. I want my revelation to empower you to really live according to my plans and purposes. Continue to seek my wisdom. I promise to give it generously to you when you ask. That wisdom will always be rooted and grounded in your reverence and awe for me. No true wisdom originates apart from me.

Humility that comes from embracing the reality that I am God (and you are not) is the foundation of wisdom. This brings you joy, peace, trust in me, and patience in the painful, arduous places.

As you obey my commandments, your wisdom will grow. You will witness how my ways are right, good and true. You tend to make foolish choices when you believe your ability to choose is better than mine.

I have flawless wisdom (soundness of action and decision-making) because I am God and have eternal experience, limitless knowledge and perfect judgment. And I am willing to share that wisdom with you as you walk with me.

I love you,
Abba

PROMISED TO YOUR PATH

How does God want me to serve?

PRAYERFUL AND PROACTIVE

"But we prayed to our God and guarded the city day and night to protect ourselves." "When you hear the blast of the trumpet, rush to wherever it is sounding. Then our God will fight for us!" NEHEMIAH 4:9, 20

My Abba,

When I read the book of Nehemiah today, these two verses stood out. I love how they show both dependence and action.

As your people faithfully rebuilt the wall around Jerusalem and faced threats from their enemies, it seems they were both prayerful and proactive. Their protection was something in which they participated. It doesn't sound like they expected endless peaceful evenings safely snuggling in robes and slippers in front of cozy fires, sipping fig cider, and cheering you on to victory.

They requested protection from you and guarded their city day and night. They rushed toward the trumpet blast and trusted you to fight for them.

Reading this today reminds me I need more practice at being prayerful and proactive. In my formative years, I didn't talk to you because I didn't know you. I stayed disconnected from myself because of the pain of abuse I could not escape. I believed early on I could not make a difference in my story. Guarding my city (protecting myself) was impossible. I could not fight. I could not flee. I had only two options — pleasing or freezing. Now I do have choices. My rag doll strategy is not necessary or helpful anymore. I want to pray and act.

As Parkinson's disease diminishes my physical and cognitive skills, my dependence on you increases. But, still, you don't magically place the words on the page. You empower me to think,

breathe, create, write, and perform a thousand other crucial functions. But I still have to choose to connect with you, sit at the computer, meditate on the passage, and type the words. You give me the choice to participate or not.

Sometimes when people say things like, "Let go and let God," it sounds to me like they are suggesting we just sit paralyzed in our puddles while we "let" you do everything for our world and us. That popular phrase only resonates with me, if it means trusting you to change something I can't. Appreciating your power and my need for it. Recognizing you are ultimately the one in control of the universe. Acknowledging you, my Creator, as truly the only one who should be in charge of my life.

Please show me how to partner with you today in my little corner of the galaxy. I know you don't need my help, but thank you for empowering me to participate.

I love you,
Mollie

My Child,

Being prayerful and proactive is especially transformative for you. Because of your history, you have swayed between taking charge in your own strength and being utterly immobilized. Neither of those options are my best for you.

I want to empower you in your weakness to walk with me. I want to give you everything you need to make a difference in this world. I want to liberate your heart so I can show my love to others through you. I want to equip you to soar on the currents of my grace, truth and love.

You are not my lifeless puppet. You have choices. Through my Spirit, you can move while at rest, take action and be still. You are not trapped without options. And I have not left you to take care of things on your own. Ask and act. If you are willing, I can give you the power to live prayerfully and proactively.

I love you,
Abba

MAKING ME RICH

"They are being tested by many troubles, and they are very poor. But they are also filled with abundant joy, which has overflowed in rich generosity." 2 CORINTHIANS 8:2

My Abba,

The world's wisdom tells me to be sensible about the way I give. But the believers described in this passage gave when earthly resources were scant and suffering was plentiful. What equipped them to give in the midst of severe trial? That kind of supernatural generosity only seems to happen when your abundant joy overpowers the pain and poverty in our lives. Then we can give generously as you lead us to, no matter what our circumstance.

I don't want my giving to be fueled by my brokenness. That kind of giving wears me out. Please make me sensitive to your direction. Let me spend myself wisely in strategic ways for your kingdom.

I have only the slightest glimpse of the ways you give to me. I think of how my husband and I have sacrificed for our children. Like most children, they don't realize what we have given up. Sleep, time, conveniences, brain cells, money, sanity, and so much more for them. And our sacrifice is nothing compared to yours.

I have ached when, sometimes, they acted ungratefully. But it is not just because I always want them to be lovely, appreciative human beings. I think it is also that their attitudes make me uncomfortable because they give me a clearer sense of my ingratitude toward you.

Please forgive me when my heart wanders down that path. I can get so focused on what I think I might want next and fail to thank you for the extraordinary blessings you have already given me. Ingratitude breeds poverty in my spirit.

GENEROUS: showing a readiness to give more of something, as in money or time, than is strictly necessary or expected   RICH: having the properties necessary to produce fertile growth

Thank you for all the ways you have sacrificed and provided for me. Please empower me to live my life generously, in gratitude and overflowing joy.

I love you,
Mollie

My Child,

When you are tested by troubles and are in need, you will still find great joy in being generous. I am generous, and you are made in my image. As you walk in my power, I will cause my joy to overflow in you as generosity. The joy you find in me coupled with your awareness of your lack is a match made in heaven.

Don't share from what you think you can logically afford to give of your time, energy, talents, resources and money. Give yourself to me and to others emotionally, spiritually, physically and financially based on how I lead you. I won't ask you to give something away I have not supplied.

When the embers of your energy are cold and dark, I am your brilliant blaze. When your heart's reservoir is dusty dry, I am your vigorous wellspring. When your soul light feels pale and feeble, I am your dazzling illumination.

Don't see your service as something that is "strictly necessary" because of the expectations of others. The gift of generosity is so much more than duty. I desire for you to experience my supernaturally inspired, empowered giving. That service will never suffocate you. You have said many times, "You have to put on your own oxygen mask first, before you can help others."

But remember, I am your oxygen. Breathe. Deeply. Instead of taking "me time," I want you to take "we time." That time for you and me will refresh, restore, and build you up.

Then, you will be rich! Your soul will be saturated with my grace, joy and love. Through me, you will have what is necessary to help produce fertile growth in others. That is the exuberant, rich life for which I created you.

I love you,
Abba

BAGS OF GOLD

"After a long time their master returned
from his trip and called them to give an account
of how they had used his money. The servant
to whom he had entrusted the five bags of gold said,
'Master, you gave me five bags of silver to invest,
and I have earned five more.' The master was
full of praise. 'Well done, my good and faithful servant.
You have been faithful in handling this small amount,
so now I will give you many more responsibilities.
Let's celebrate together!'"
MATTHEW 25:19–21

My Abba,

I can embrace your perfect fairness, faithfulness, and graciousness as my master. Your flawless traits give me absolute security. I am not worried about a lack of discernment on your part as you look at how I use what you have given me.

But then there is me. Clearly, I have not always been a consistent steward of certain gifts you have chosen to give me. Things that come to mind are: gifts of expression (like teaching or writing), money, possessions, time, and some relationships with friends and family. I don't always invest your currency well. I am sorry.

As you entrust me with your priceless "bags of gold," please give me the desire and the power to expend them well.

I want to be a servant who is led by your priorities and invests extravagantly and wisely for you. Please show me what that looks like. Give me a heart that is exquisitely sensitive to your leading. I know the currency of each day is a gift.

Help me to invest all that you give me today in a way that makes you smile.

I love you,
Mollie

My Child,

I am so glad you want to please me. How you invest the gifts I entrust to you is important. All good gifts come from me. Even your time is a gift — with an expiration date. There are so many priorities vying for your attention, you can get lost in the dense thicket of choices.

I want to give you my matchless vision for how all your gifts can be used in greater ways. That will not always look grand to you or others. But trust me, I have a real eye for this kind of thing.

> *"Imagine the joy of crossing the finish line as I exclaim, 'Well done, my good and faithful servant!'"*

You want me to be "full of praise" when I look at you. You desire my approval for your investments. That is good. Remember, I will always approve of who you are because Christ has reconciled us (made right what was wrong between us). When I look at you, I see his perfect righteousness.

But there is always room for improvement in how you invest. Sometimes fear of failure is your enemy. You would like a scientifically proven, well-woven safety net, in case you slip, as you walk the tightrope over a particularly deep canyon.

Sometimes fear of discomfort keeps you from investing well. When you invest well, you can find yourself plunging down the more difficult slope. It is worth it. I am worth it. And I am with you, even when you hit that icy, rocky patch moving way too fast.

I want you to be faithful in the small things so I can increase your responsibilities. At day's end, I want to celebrate with you because you have chosen to invest yourself well.

Anything you do empowered by my Spirit will make me smile. You don't have to do it perfectly. I just want to be with you in the thick of it, infusing you with my gifts and power, while cheering you on. Imagine the joy of crossing the finish line as I exclaim, "Well done, my good and faithful servant!"

I love you,
Abba

THE MOMENT HE KNOCKS

"Be dressed for service and keep your lamps burning as though you were waiting on your master to return from the wedding feast. Then you will be ready to open the door and let him in the moment he arrives and knocks." LUKE 12:35–36

My Child,

As you ponder these definitions, I have some questions for you to consider, also.

Are you ready to serve me? Have you spent time with me, allowing me to get your heart and mind prepared? In your own strength, you will not cultivate the sensitivity to my Spirit needed to serve me well. But I can create an eager responsiveness in you, if you are willing.

Are you available for immediate use or too busy or distracted with your own schedule and agenda? Being available for immediate use by me takes cultivation of a tender heart, focus and planning. The world, our enemy and your flesh can steal your availability without a moment's notice, if you allow it.

Are you keen or quick to give yourself to me and what I have for you? Do you truly want to glorify me more than you want the lesser things? In the times when you find yourself playing in the mud with your trinkets, call my name. I will lift you up, wash you off, and show you the path I have for you.

Do you realize your endless need for my presence? Do you hunger and thirst to participate with me in my kingdom purposes?

READY: in a suitable or right state for an activity, action, or situation, fully prepared; available for immediate use; keen or quick to give; in need of, eager, or having a desire for; inclined, willing to do something, in such a condition as to be likely to do something

I can position your heart and mind so you are inclined and willing to walk in my ways. Are you ready?

I love you,
Abba

My Abba,

These truths remind me of those recurring nightmares I have in which I am not prepared for the test, dressed for the speech, or ready to turn in the paper. Convinced my night musings are reality, I wake up distraught.

Obviously, being dressed for service and well prepared is something I need to explore.

Sometimes when you invite me to participate in something you are doing, I think I am ready. I have noticed, though, if there is a special event, I am better at the preparation. It is the daily readiness I lack. Everyday rhythms can sing my readiness to sleep.

So what are the things I do to be well prepared to serve at a special event?

I ask for you to speak into my process, guide me, empower me, and give me your wisdom, peace, and everything else I need to be ready.

I listen, think and plan. I set aside as many things as I can that do not help me focus and get ready. I enlist the help of others.

Please give me the power to make these practices part of my daily routine. Although I know you are always with me, wake me up to your presence, plans and purposes each day. I want to be ready to open the door and let you in the moment you knock.

I love you,
Mollie

GIFTS FOR MY ENEMIES

"But love your enemies, do good to them, and lend to them without expecting to get anything back. Then your reward will be great, and you will be children of the Most High, because he is kind to the ungrateful and wicked. Be merciful, just as your Father is merciful."
LUKE 6:35–36

My Child,

Empowered by my Spirit, you can offer your enemies the gifts of generosity, kindness, forgiveness, and mercy. I can show you how to love your enemies well and do good in their lives. This does not mean always giving everyone everything they want. It is important for you to follow my lead. I am the only one who completely understands what is good.

Sometimes you will never have contact with an enemy, but you can fervently intercede for that person to come into an ever deepening, life-giving relationship with me. That is the greatest gift you can give them.

Be sure you are not looking for something in return. That is never my motive when I do good in your life. Your reward will be great when you show love to your enemies, but I don't want that to be what drives your behavior. You are my child. I want you to act like me.

> *"I don't struggle with a scarcity of resources. My supplies are endless."*

Remember, every kindness I extend is toward someone who doesn't deserve it. I love those who are ungrateful and wicked, just like you are at times. I want you to be merciful, just as I am merciful.

I want you to give without fear of lack. My gifts are boundless. You can never outgive me. My warehouse is never empty. I don't struggle with a scarcity of resources. My supplies are endless. I want to lavish them on you and delight in you as you lavish them on others.

I love you,
Abba

My Abba,

I love the quote I found this morning from Dave Willis as I was pondering this topic. "Don't treat people the way they treat you; treat them the way God treats you."

Show me more about how to treat people who don't treat me well. I want to make that decision in light of my dependence on your infinite resources. I cannot even pretend to do this in my own strength. I don't want to give to others to feed some nagging need in my soul. Serving others out of my woundedness is like trying to offer refreshment from a scorched gully.

I want to make a divine sacrifice empowered by your Spirit. Sometimes, though, I think what looks like a good or kind act is not the loving thing for me to do. Please teach me more about sanctified sacrifice. Show me what is truly in someone's best interest.

If you are kind to those who are ungrateful and wicked, then I know I should be too. I just need to know when a course of action is wisdom from you and when it is spawned from my wounds or our culture's latest psychobabble.

You detest sin but remain devoted to the sinner. I need your power to do the same. I want to love and do good to those whose actions I find really annoying, offensive, or particularly evil. Give me your love for others so I act like a child of the Most High God.

Please grant me everything I need — the grace, goodness, wisdom and mercy — to love like you love and give like you give.

I love you,
Mollie

PROMISED TO YOUR PATH

"One day as these men were worshiping the Lord and fasting, the Holy Spirit said, 'Dedicate Barnabas and Saul for the special work I have for them.' So after more fasting and prayer, the men laid their hands on them and sent them on their way."
ACTS 13:2–3

My Abba,

The word "dedicate" captures my attention this morning. What did it mean when you asked these people to "dedicate Barnabas and Saul for the special work" you had for them? It seems, after looking at some meanings, that you wanted them devoted, given, set apart, committed, promised to a particular purpose.

I want a heart that is prepared through time in the Scriptures, worship, fasting, and prayer to understand the particular task or purpose you have for me. I want to devote myself to what is on your heart. I can think of a million good (and not so good) ways to spend my time today. But I want to sense your heartbeat.

Your path for me is always rich. Sometimes it is a treacherous, rocky trail on the precipice of a hungry chasm. (Our mule ride traversing the cliffs in Molokai comes to mind.) Other times your path feels gentle and quiet like a morning walk between majestic pines in a lush forest. But no matter what, your path brings life. Help me take your hand and follow you today.

DEDICATE: to set apart, to devote (time, effort, or oneself) to a particular task or purpose   DEVOTE: to give all or a large part of one's time or resources to a person, activity or cause, to persist in adherence to someone or something; to be intently engaged in, attend constantly to, to undertake resolutely, to practice diligently

Please make me persistently, resolutely, and diligently dedicated to you and your purposes.

I love you,
Mollie

My Child,

You are beginning to understand that our connection on this journey is more important than the scenery. You know what it is like to enjoy the company of a loved one so much that you don't really care where you are. That is how it can be for us.

> *"Home is where I am.*
> *And I am always with you."*

I know you love the quiet walk in the forest. But sometimes you will need to cling to me on the precipice. I have set you apart for a specific journey with me. It won't look like your neighbor's. My plans for you are as singular as your DNA.

Our connection is also unique. Our relationship will never be duplicated. Cherish our one-of-a-kind, priceless connection. The more you invest in it, the richer it will become. I am already fully committed — all in.

Our communion can outshine all of the circumstances you will encounter today. Don't worry about where you will wind up at nightfall. Home is where I am. And I am always with you.

Although you won't always be ebullient about your surroundings on your journey, just remember enduring joy comes from the greatest gift of all — eternal relationship with me. As you spend yourself on our connection, you will find joy, whether you are drifting through quiet forests or wrestling on a rocky precipice.

I love you,
Abba

STRIKE A CHORD

"Live in harmony with each other. Don't be too proud to enjoy the company of ordinary people. And don't think you know it all!" ROMANS 12:16

"May God, who gives this patience and encouragement, help you live in complete harmony with each other, as is fitting for followers of Christ Jesus." ROMANS 15:5

"Above all, clothe yourselves with love, which binds us all together in perfect harmony." COLOSSIANS 3:14

My Child,

I want your brothers, sisters and you to prioritize harmony. Not all your ideas, preferences, goals and desires will be exactly the same. I didn't design everyone to play the same note. But our forever family can make beautiful, pleasing music with the supernatural power to dispel hate and strife.

If you rely on my Spirit to empower your connections with your brothers and sisters, you can be part of a luminous love song that dismantles the darkness. My love can bind you together in the most captivating chords.

Each note in a chord performs an integral part. Your note is not more, or less important, than anyone else's. Both pride and false humility are harmony busters. Never look down on your, or another's, sound. Diversity in the notes contributes to the rich beauty of the music I am making.

Remember the way an orchestra sounds when it is warming up. Until the conductor takes his place, gifted musicians can sound off

---

HARMONY: the quality of forming a pleasing whole; the combination of musical notes in a chord having a pleasing effect

beat, off key, and chaotic. I am your Conductor. Follow me and enjoy my glorious symphony.

I love you,
Abba

My Abba,

I realize this weekend I contributed to dissonance. Please forgive me. At our family gathering, I became so focused on being absolved from blame, I lost sight of your song.

Sometimes I experience the emotions of an overgrown third grader when immersed in my family of origin. I don't know if I was flat or sharp, but I was definitely playing the wrong notes.

> *"you can be part of a luminous love song that dismantles the darkness"*

I used to be a desperate peacemaker at all costs, even when it was not right or healthy for others or me. I don't want to go back to that unhealthy practice. I need more skill and experience at speaking the truth in love when there is conflict. Since I hate conflict, it makes me itch to admit this. Practicing skillful conflict resolution sounds akin to a bad case of chickenpox.

Even so, I want to learn to live in harmony. Please show me the art of contributing to unity, even when there is discord that needs to be resolved. Make me a truth-teller motivated by your love.

The longer I walk with you, the more opportunities you give me to tackle the really difficult relational stuff. I am glad you haven't left me to my own devices. Without your intervention, I might still be banging out the few monotonous notes of "Mary Had a Little Lamb" I learned as a child.

But with these more complex compositions, I need your constant direction. Thank you for your patience and encouragement. Clothe me in your love so I may live in a manner fitting for a follower of Christ Jesus.

I love you,
Mollie

SUPERFOOD

"Beloved, let's love one another;
for love is from God"
1 JOHN 4:7a

"Love is patient, love is kind, it is not jealous;
love does not brag, it is not arrogant. It does not
act disgracefully, it does not seek its own benefit;
it is not provoked, does not keep an account of
a wrong suffered, it does not rejoice in unrighteousness,
but rejoices with the truth; it keeps every confidence,
it believes all things, hopes all things, endures all things."
1 CORINTHIANS 13:4-7

My Child,

Seek my highest calling in all things. I call you to love. Without love, everything you do today, or any day, will be meaningless.

I am love. You are my child, so I want you to be like me. I want our family resemblance to be apparent. I am patient and kind. I am not proud or rude. I am not irritable with you. I do not keep a record of the ways you have wronged others and me. I will never give up on you.

I always rejoice in justice and truth. Love does not mean I just tell you what you want to hear. My love is steeped in truth. It is not loving to lie to someone. My love is perfect and eternal, enduring through every season and circumstance.

All the gifts, talents, and accomplishments that people revere will be useless in eternity. Special abilities and knowledge will not last. Put away the childish priorities in your life and focus on what will endure.

Love me. Love those I have put around you. Set your heart and mind on what transcends these fleeting days on earth.

I love you,
Abba

My Abba,

It saddens me when I ignore opportunities to enjoy your love for me. I miss out, and then, others do also. With an empty tank, I do not love the people in my life very well. Sometimes, I neglect those divine delicacies on my plate because I am distracted by the junk food across the table.

This time of isolation during the pandemic, with only a few family members, gives my unlovely attitudes no place to run for cover. You say, "Love is patient." How much of my impatience (in the past) has been disguised by my freedom to change my scenery when my composure frays at the edges?

You say love "does not seek its own benefit." Does my self-interest currently feel agitated by my lack of latitude to choose freely? I am used to living with limitations, but this unexpected, formidable gale is stretching my, already, taut sails.

You say love "is not provoked." My typically calm soul feels disrupted. It's like someone is incessantly skipping pebbles across the placid waters of my well-being. I think I may be more tempted to keep a record of my loved ones' wrongs while we are corralled in close quarters.

Forgive me for the times I have failed to love you and others well. I can't love people well in my own strength. Please love them through me. Give me the supernatural sense to jealously guard the richest of foods — to live in your endless love.

When I indulge in empty calories, I start to lose my appetite for what is truly nourishing. (What you offer is like eternal superfood.) I can get fixated on something that will not be important by tomorrow — much less a year from now. Don't let me mindlessly swallow this lie.

Please make me ravenous for your love today. Let my hunger for you and your love inspire all my choices.

I love you,
Mollie

MAKE US ONE

"And the world hates them because they do not belong to the world, just as I do not belong to the world. I'm not asking you to take them out of the world, but to keep them safe from the evil one. They do not belong to this world any more than I do."

"I am praying not only for these disciples but also for all who will ever believe in me through their message. I pray that they will all be one, just as you and I are one—as you are in me, Father, and I am in you. And may they be in us so that the world will believe you sent me. I have given them the glory you gave me, so they may be one as we are one. I am in them and you are in me. May they experience such perfect unity that the world will know that you sent me and that you love them as much as you love me."
JOHN 17:14–16, 20–23

My Child,

You belong to me and were created to bring me glory. Don't entertain anyone else's false claim to you. You are mine and protected by the power of my name. You are joined to me.

The world will hate you because I am in you and it hates me. Because you don't belong to this world, you can feel like an outcast if your overwhelming desire is to fit in. I don't need you to fit in. I want you to be set apart for my service. I made you holy (set apart) by my sacrifice for you. I took care of that because you couldn't do it for yourself, no matter how hard you tried.

Just as the Spirit, Son and I are one, I want you to be one with us and others who know me. Because I bless you with my radiant beauty (glory), you are united with others who follow me and carry my glory.

That unity will show the world I am God and have the power to supernaturally knit together human hearts with the magnificent threads of my love.

I love you,
Abba

My Abba,

Much of my life, I felt like an outsider trying to be acceptable enough to earn my way in. Thank you for bringing healing to my heart as you have shown me my grace-filled place in your forever family. And thank you for reminding me it is futile to try to gain the acceptance of people who reject me because I belong to you. I would never trade their acceptance for the indescribable joy of belonging to you, the God of the Galaxies — the King of Kings — the Lord of Lords!

What other belonging do I need? I rejoice today that you have made me yours and created me to bring you glory. Give me the power to point to your perfection.

Thank you for your protection from our enemy. I know I am joined to you forever and I can never be taken away from you. That is the greatest way you protect me — by protecting me from an eternity apart from you. Thank you for making me holy by your sacrifice so that I can always be with you.

"you have shown me my grace-filled place in your forever family"

I want to live in unity with the others who love you and carry your glory. I cannot do this apart from the power of your Spirit. Despite our redemption, we are still an unruly band of misfits who would probably not be interested in each other, unless you intervened. Cause us to be drawn to your beauty in each other. Give us the unconditional love for one another that you experience in the Trinity.

I love you,
Mollie

DIFFICULT ONES

"We urge you, brothers and sisters, admonish the unruly, encourage the fainthearted, help the weak, be patient with everyone." 1 THESSALONIANS 5:14

My Abba,

This truth implores me to love people in ways that stretch my heart, soul, mind and strength. It reminds me how I struggle with some of the rowdy demands of helping those in need.

I remember my friend (a pastor) joking once, "Ministry would be great, if it weren't for the people!" I laughed at his irony but thought he was a bit serious. I felt sad for him and a little smug in my self-assurance that I would simply feel grateful for anyone God wanted me to help. (Yes, I was young and excessively optimistic about my way of being in the world.)

As decades have passed, to my chagrin, I have discovered I actually do want people to be less … problematic. I sometimes internally cringe when working with some of (what I consider) the difficult people. I tend to favor encouraging the disheartened and helping the weak, but not so much, serving the critical, confrontational, legalistic, disruptive or annoying types.

How can this be? I lead a recovery ministry. Shouldn't I feel drawn to the difficult folks? The head-in-the-sand ones who avoid working on their own issues because life would be perfect if their loved ones would just change? The embarrassing, inappropriate ones with the stunted social skills of a 12-year-old boy awkwardly trapped in pre-pubescence? The desperately insecure ones who feign egos as big as a West Texas sky and tell you all the ways you are doing things wrong?

If I acknowledge reality, I am inclined to gravitate toward those who are struggling in a way that allows them to be somewhat congenial while growing and healing. Please forgive me.

I do not love everyone in my life unconditionally. But I want to. Please love them through me. I am not able to do this on my own. And, please, continually remind me I am not in charge of fixing anyone — especially not to fashion them in a way that is more pleasing to me.

Thank you that you never give up on me when I am one of the difficult people. I am grateful you love me, even when I am most unlovable.

I love you,
Mollie

My Child,

Some people's flaws and failings are more palatable to you than others. For the most part, you better tolerate peculiarities and character defects that don't push on your wounds. Aggressive, critical behaviors trigger you.

As you have become more adept at depending on me, you have gained greater resilience. You have stopped looking at people through rose-colored glasses. Now, more than not, you don't try to paint over poor behavior. These are crucial steps. I can't help you, if you don't walk with me in reality.

"By the power of my Spirit, you can love even the difficult ones, because I do."

You are more in tune with your emotions and more honest about how people affect you. These are good things. You can't heal a wound by saying it's not there. But don't stop there. I want you to bring me the uncomfortable emotions you feel when dealing with hostile, disapproving people.

My perfect, infinite, forever love can bring healing to all the faulty ways people try to cope with life. I can fill your heart with my unconditional love. By the power of my Spirit, you can love even the difficult ones, because I do.

I love you,
Abba

IGNITE OUR SOULS

"Let's hold firmly to the confession of our hope without wavering, for He who promised is faithful; and let's consider how to encourage one another in love and good deeds, not abandoning our own meeting together, as is the habit of some people, but encouraging one another; and all the more as you see the day drawing near." HEBREWS 10: 23–25

My Child,

Hold tightly to your hope in me. I am worth it. The more time we spend together in deepening connection, the more you will desire my flawlessly faithful company.

I know you have dealt with a lot of duplicity and deception in your life. Humans can be that way. I cannot. My words are always right, true and life-giving. Listen as I sing my love song over your heart today.

As you walk with others, inspire them by sharing our love story. Constantly remind them that I love them also with a perfect, infinite, eternal love. I am eager to pursue a fervent relationship with each one I have created. Encourage one another with this truth.

For my body of believers to move gracefully in the good deeds I have choreographed for you, the hands and feet must move in rhythm with the arms and legs. This only happens by the power of my Spirit and through your dedication to practice.

You all need continuous experience at moving in unison under my direction, accomplishing my plans and purposes. Commit steadfastly to me and one another. You cannot imagine the beauty we will create together.

I love you,
Abba

My Abba,

Thank you for caring for me so tenderly. Thank you for giving me a deep desire for your presence, but also for recognizing my frailty. Thank you for your perfect faithfulness to me in my weakness.

Show me powerful ways to love and encourage the people you place on my path. Sometimes I grow weary of learning to live well with others. My self-centered tendencies paired with their less-than-graceful steps can create a disjointed dance, instead of the inspiring waltz you just described. Forgive me.

"Ignite our souls with your song."

During this time of social distancing, sometimes the "meeting together" has taken some creativity. Please don't let us lose heart. I know the church has had many formidable challenges to cohesive fellowship over the centuries, but you have still brought supernatural unity. Knit our hearts closer together, even when we may not physically be together.

Please make our hearts burn for you, your people, plans and purposes. I want us to dance to the melody for which you designed us. Ignite our souls with your song. Please show us your steps and give us the power to follow your lead.

I love you,
Mollie

LOVE WITH LEGS

"Jesus, knowing that the Father had handed all things over to Him, and that He had come forth from God and was going back to God, got up from supper and laid His outer garments aside; and He took a towel and tied it around Himself. Then He poured water into the basin, and began washing the disciples' feet and wiping them with the towel which He had tied around Himself."

"Then, when He had washed their feet, and taken His garments and reclined at the table again, He said to them, 'Do you know what I have done for you? You call Me "Teacher" and "Lord"; and you are correct, for so I am. So if I, the Lord and the Teacher, washed your feet, you also ought to wash one another's feet. For I gave you an example, so that you also would do just as I did for you. Truly, truly I say to you, a slave is not greater than his master, nor is one who is sent greater than the one who sent him. If you know these things, you are blessed if you do them.'"
JOHN 13:3–5, 12–17

My Child,

My Son was fully aware of who he was when he entered into this humble act of service. He knew he had unlimited power. He knew he came from me, was returning to me, and was God. And yet, he chose to serve those he created.

He took on the most menial of human tasks — washing feet. He left his meal, prepared for the job, and humbled himself to illustrate

true service. Christ has set the example. Do you want to follow him and serve in that way?

Do you find it difficult to get your hands dirty and do what is considered lowly? You know those sacrificial acts when you wind up worn out, sweaty, grimy, and under-appreciated by those you serve?

Sometimes you feel certain tasks are trivial or insignificant. But I can give you a heart that desires to serve as Christ did, in the momentous and the menial.

If you are truly confident in whom I created you to be, you will not chafe in the least lofty of tasks. Anything done empowered by my Spirit has eternal value. I am right there with you in the middle of the mess.

I love you,
Abba

My Abba,

I am so glad to be reminded of your truth on service. I realize I feel fulfilled when I serve through teaching, leading or writing. For nine years, I have been focused on leading a ministry that is demanding but definitely rewarding.

Now the "social distancing" we are practicing with the corona virus raging around our planet is giving me more opportunities to serve in the quiet recesses of our home. With multiple family members who are at high risk for serious outcomes if they contract the disease, you have presented me with new opportunities to serve.

I admit sanitizing surfaces, tending to laundry, and clearing daily clutter that seems to reinvent itself every hour is not my preferred jam. But here I am. You are patiently reminding me of the blessing of humble tasks as I serve behind the scenes with only you watching.

Thank you for the strong reminder of the way you, the God of the Galaxies, serve us. That earth-shaking reality consumes my pride. If you do what you do, what task is beneath me? Continue to teach me how to love and serve graciously (in grand and modest ways). I want my love to have legs.

Please make me a conduit of your love. Flow through me to others in a way that causes them to understand it is your love that they are experiencing.

I love you,
Mollie

CAUGHT UP IN YOUR SYMPHONY

"I am not asking on behalf of these alone, but also for those who believe in Me through their word, that they may all be one; just as You, Father, are in Me and I in You, that they also may be in Us, so that the world may believe that You sent Me."
JOHN 17:20–21

My Child,

You believed in me through the message of my Son. You are now a vital member of our family. No one can ever take your place. Although our family is large, I will never create another just like you.

Take up the unique role in our family that I designed for you. By the power of my Spirit, I can accomplish my glorious purposes through you. Sit and soak in my presence, so you may serve in my power.

I desire for you to be caught up in the symphony I am writing. I have perfect harmony with my Spirit and Son. I want you also to enjoy that beautiful music with your forever family and me.

Quickly set aside things that create discord. As my glorious love song rises up in my children, others will be drawn to me. I love you just as I love my Son. I love you perfectly and unconditionally. It is not possible for me to love you any other way.

Play in the light of my love today. Encourage your brothers and sisters to join in. The world is so hungry for my music.

I love you,
Abba

My Abba,

You always know just what I need. I want to be captivated by your music today. Please still my heart and mind and draw me into your eternal melody. The unity you describe in the Trinity is what I want to experience with you and others. I want to be one with you and your children.

I am thinking about when a young child repetitively hits a single note on a piano. After a while, it can make the listener feel a bit crazy. Not exactly engaging. But it doesn't make that one note wrong or "less than." If that note becomes a part of a chord and is placed in a score with other beautiful chords to create magnificent harmony, everything changes. That note could become part of a work of art that blesses hearts and minds for generations.

I don't want to just stand alone playing my one note. I want to be part of your eternal chorus. Show me how to join in your glorious song and enjoy the matchless pleasure of our unity.

With my brothers and sisters, let me enter into the delightful celebration of you, which you orchestrated before the beginning of time. I want to play my instrument in your opus. I know we don't all play the same instrument or, even, the same notes. But when we play our parts and are in tune with you, your symphony is breathtaking.

I love you,
Mollie

FRAGRANT DAYS

How do I deepen my delight in God?

UNVEILED

"But whenever anyone turns to the Lord, the veil is taken away. Now the Lord is the Spirit, and where the Spirit of the Lord is, there is freedom. And we all, who with unveiled faces contemplate the Lord's glory, are being transformed into his image with ever-increasing glory, which comes from the Lord, who is the Spirit."
2 CORINTHIANS 3:16–18

My Abba,

Thank you for removing the veil over my heart and coming to live in me. Your glorious presence broke through the demanding, dense clouds that threatened to consume my horizon.

Thank you for the peerless opportunity of becoming more like you. Me (fragile, failing child of dust) becoming a bit more like you (perfect, beautiful and eternal God).

"Please keep pouring light in me until all is shimmering."

I find these meanings of "contemplate" encouraging. Thank you for transforming me as I look thoughtfully at you for a long time, think profoundly about you, meditate on you, and create more "open space" to observe who you are. I know focused time with you each day in prayer, worship, and your Word changes me in a profound way.

I can experience your dazzling love as it overflows in me. Or, I can allow my sin to shroud my heart so your presence is obscured in me. When I see it that way, the choice seems inescapably clear.

CONTEMPLATE: *look at thoughtfully for a long time; think profoundly about and at length; look at with continued attention, meditate, Latin templum, "open space for observation"*

Please keep pouring light in me until all is shimmering. Make me an illuminated beacon of your love, grace and freedom today.

I love you,
Mollie

My Child,

You could never find life in those dreary grave clothes. When you turned to me, I infused you with my life, hope and love so you could leave the dead things behind. I am the God of your radiant transformation.

I can give you unwavering confidence in me when you find yourself in the gridlock of circumstances. I have all the power you lack. I can invigorate you, so that you are not just surviving, but thriving.

When your new life began, I gave you freedom from the tyranny of sin and death. And now you, who with an unveiled face contemplate and reflect my glory, are being transformed into my likeness with my glory ever-increasing in you.

That is my gift to you each day you walk with me. It is the supernatural fruit of the intimate connection I forged with you. Your future is bright, no matter what may come, because I, the God of Luminosity, have made my home in your heart.

I love you,
Abba

WITH OR WITHOUT WORDS

"One of the Pharisees asked Jesus to have dinner with him, so Jesus went to his home and sat down to eat. When a certain immoral woman from that city heard he was eating there, she brought a beautiful alabaster jar filled with expensive perfume. Then she knelt behind him at his feet, weeping. Her tears fell on his feet, and she wiped them off with her hair. Then she kept kissing his feet and putting perfume on them."
LUKE 7:36–38

My Child,

This woman's sins were glaringly obvious in her town. The self-righteous crowd at that dinner would have never welcomed her. But she did not prioritize convention or pretense.

She was not there to make a civilized gesture of thanks. She knew people would talk about her "ridiculous" behavior. But the landslide of her love for Christ muffled any shred of propriety she still possessed. The gesture was financially costly for her, also. In order to worship my Son in this way, she was willing to give up the comforts that valuable possession could have afforded her, if she had kept it for herself.

She didn't go in with a safety net. She knew she would be reviled by the "good" people. She kept her gaze solely on Jesus despite the pounding disapproval that dominated the room. She profoundly humbled herself in this act of worship. Instead of using water and a rag, as a slave would to wash Jesus's feet, she utilized the deluge of her tears and her own hair.

WORSHIP: the expression of devotion and adoration
DEVOTE: to give all or a large part of one's time or resources to

And then taking it a step further, she anointed him with the sacrificial gift of expensive perfume and countless kisses. She gave her whole heart. True passion for me is that way. You don't ration it for another day. Gratitude, joy and love overwhelmed her. Nothing could stand in the way of her expressing that. She used everything she had to demonstrate the reality of her love.

You, too, will thrive at my feet. Worship me with wild abandon — through sacrifice, tears, humility, and joy. The delight of my presence will mute the voice of your inhibition, practicality, and pride. Celebrate me there in that silence.

I love you,
Abba

My Abba,

I am never as joyful as when I worship you with untamed devotion — consumed with my desire for your presence. In that space, the world sputters out and time stands still.

More than not, I enter into that sacred place when I am most desperate for connection with you. Many times, that is when I find myself near the bottom of a dismal pit and my dime store treasures don't sparkle in the dark. Please forgive me. I don't want to wait for disturbing circumstances to morph my lukewarm desire into desperation before I devote myself to fervently seeking connection with you. Please give me a passion for your presence every day.

Remind me daily what a breathtaking opportunity it is to enjoy a relationship with you. Please don't let me look away. I realize my worship (expressing devotion and adoration) is not just about singing songs to you. The woman in this passage did not utter a word.

> *"In that space,*
> *the world sputters out and*
> *time stands still."*

Thanks for prompting me to remember that my devotion to you can be expressed with my thoughts, desires, attitudes, voice, and actions. I can worship you in song, deed, and without moving or making a sound.

Worship is what I am created for. It is my forever calling! There is nothing as freeing as worshiping you. I want everything in my life to flow from my adoration of you — when it seems costly and when it does not.

I love you,
Mollie

COME ON IN

"The one thing I ask of the Lord — the thing I seek most — is to live in the house of the Lord all the days of my life, delighting in the Lord's perfections and meditating in his temple." PSALM 27:4

My Abba,

Even as I try to still myself to focus on the one thing I know will bring me the greatest pleasure, my mind darts through my to-do list like a neurotic rabbit. I have tasted and seen how good you are and how amazing it is to focus on your beauty. I have spent hours in the past overcome by the joy of your presence as I meditated on you.

Ignorance is not my excuse.

"Awe me with your matchless colors and light today, as I delight in your perfections."

Enjoying my time with you reminds me of getting into my favorite icy swimming hole — Barton Springs. There is always a bit of angst before, and during, my descent into that chilly water. Most every time, there is a point when I question my mental health.

For a moment, I am convinced. Certainly this is not practical, wise, or sane. Especially in the winter, when I might be the only human in the pool. This cannot be good for me! In addition, it takes too much time and keeps me from getting "real" things done.

But within a few minutes, I swim into reality.

Dazzling light rushes before me like a luminous herd of wild horses racing across a fluid field of blues and greens. I become exuberant — in awe of the experience. Pain fades. I feel so alive

---

DELIGHTING: *taking great pleasure*   MEDITATING: *thinking deeply or focusing one's mind for a period of time*

and free as I slide quietly through the water. About that time (with a smile I can't subdue on my face) I whisper to myself, "What was I thinking?" I suddenly feel disappointment for all the earthbound creatures not in the water with me, clinging to their safe and familiar terrain.

Yet, all the delight I find in the water does not come close to the joy I experience in your presence. Please captivate me with your beauty as I savor who you are. Awe me with your matchless colors and light today, as I delight in your perfections.

I love you,
Mollie

My Child,

When you believe the truth about who I am, you will not struggle to get in the water. Anyone who is utterly convinced something, or someone, will please them greatly and leave them happy and satisfied, does not have to be pushed in.

The obstacles that interfere with our connection become substantial only when your perception of me is diminished. My perfection offers you the opportunity to be fulfilled and pleased as you enjoy the unparalleled waters of my presence.

This will seem counterintuitive when your day is filled with unrelenting responsibilities barking on the shoreline. Don't listen to their arguments. Those demanding bullies will always be there, trying to corral your attention.

Come on in. Trust me, the water is perfect. My springs of living water will quench that nagging thirst in your soul like nothing else can.

I love you,
Abba

DEEP ROOTS

"Then Christ will make his home in your hearts as you trust in him. Your roots will grow down into God's love and keep you strong." EPHESIANS 3:17

My Abba,

The more I trust you, the more I experience the reality of you making your home in my heart. I realize you are always there. But the more I welcome you into my daily rhythm, the more I enjoy your presence.

I don't want to tuck you away in some remote parlor (my formal living room) where I only invite special guests but never spend much time. If I relegate you to the fringes of my life, I will not take pleasure in your company the way you want me to. What a loss.

The truth is I don't want to dress up in my Sunday best and slip in superficial visits with you sandwiched in between my "important" commitments. I want to focus on you and your words so my roots will grow down deeply into your love. I know our relationship will not thrive any other way.

> *"held fast by your strength,*
> *my roots diving deeper*
> *into the solid rock of your love"*

I want the kind of relationship that is free from parlor talk. I want authentic communication. Honest-to-God response. Genuine connection. I am picturing an intimate conversation with the only One who fully knows me in front of a lively fire on my well-worn sofa in my flannel robe with a warm cup of peppermint tea. You lovingly nourish me with your truth and grace. I feel fully at home with you.

I know that vibrant connection will keep me strong. When I am grounded in your love, the inclement weather of this life does not uproot me. Though these storms are fierce, I want to be like that oak

tree in our yard. Grounded, strong, and majestic. The winds come, but it just sways gracefully.

Please make me like that. As the winds blow, I want to gracefully sway — held fast by your strength, my roots diving deeper into the solid rock of your love.

I love you,
Mollie

My Child,

You have struggled at times to feel rooted. But I am your forever home. Each day, your roots can grow ever deeper in my love. I am your stability, your place to feel grounded.

I am your constancy — the same yesterday, today, and tomorrow. I am not tossed about by circumstances. You don't have to be, either. I am your safe harbor.

I want you to be rooted and grounded in my love. Remember my love is infinitely greater than the galaxies. That infinite love will sustain you when everything else withers, diminishes and dies.

What I have in store for you will defy your imagination. We can be on an amazing adventure and at home together — all at the same time. Remember, home is where I am. Stay close. Watch what I do. I will amaze you.

I love you,
Abba

ONE THING

"As Jesus and the disciples continued on their way to Jerusalem, they came to a certain village where a woman named Martha welcomed him into her home. Her sister, Mary, sat at the Lord's feet, listening to what he taught. But Martha was distracted by the big dinner she was preparing. She came to Jesus and said, 'Lord, doesn't it seem unfair to you that my sister just sits here while I do all the work? Tell her to come and help me.'

"But the Lord said to her, 'My dear Martha, you are worried and upset over all these details! There is only one thing worth being concerned about. Mary has discovered it, and it will not be taken away from her.'"
LUKE 10:38–42

My Abba,

I don't ever want to lose sight of the joy of sitting at your feet. I don't want to be "worried and upset over all these details" of life. I want my connection with you to be my one great concern. I don't often miss feeding my body. Why would I not prioritize each day so nothing would keep me from feeding my spirit?

    First, I think it is because our enemy makes it a priority to attempt to keep me, and others who love you, from daily, meaningful communion with you. Second, I think I get caught up in what I can see. I see all the pieces of my day puffed up, banging their drums for my attention while bellowing of their importance.

    You are eternally patient and present. Not a screamer. No drums. I can get distracted by what squeals. I, also, sometimes take advantage of your gentle lovingkindness. I know you will always be here for me.

I typically have identified with Mary in the story of Mary and Martha. But there have been some days this week when I have acted like Martha ... doing, doing, done. Spent. Face down choking on the dust of my busyness left by the cavalry of my bad choices.

I don't want to live that way on any day. Ever.

I just remembered my name, Mollie, is derived from the name Mary. That is the woman I want to be. Everyday. The wise one who chooses well. The joyful one who is constantly connected to your heart. The overflowing one who is brimming with your living water — prepared for the work you have for me.

Please help me return each day to the woman you created me to be ... alive, full of joy, enamored with your presence.

I love you,
Mollie

My Child,

The hamster wheel is no place for a child of the King of Kings. It will not take you anywhere. Your life is filled with people in crisis and pain. That will never change. Follow Christ's example. Pull away from the chaos and pain and sit with me.

> *"Pull away from the chaos and pain and sit with me."*

Please don't try to pour into others with an empty cup. That won't quench anyone's thirst. I will fill your cup. As always, I want you to serve from the wellspring of our intimacy.

Devote your attention to the one thing that is more important than anything else — adoring me. That will never be taken from you. Only you can choose to give it up. You are right. I am always available. However, it does not make me less significant because I am flawlessly faithful.

You have chosen well today. Continue to be intentional and fiercely protective of our time together. It is a treasure you should guard jealously.

I love you,
Abba

STAYCATION

"Come let us worship and bow down.
Let us kneel before the Lord our maker,
for he is our God."
PSALM 95:6–7a

My Child,

Come away with me. Step away from your chores. For a moment, lay down your responsibilities. Put aside the mind clutter. Leave those commitments over there, for just a while.

Don't try to juggle all the weighty stuff of this life, while you bow down before me. You are distracted by those things that fidget and squirm like needy children trying to capture your attention. Put them down. Think of our time each day as a short vacation.

When you go on vacation, the idea is to leave behind the things that take away from rest and relaxation. You put a lot of thought into how to get the most pleasure from your vacation. I want you to plan purposely for our time, and jealously guard it the way you would when delighting in a special holiday at the seashore.

I am always perfect rest. As you enjoy my presence, you find inexplicable joy. Is there any other time when your heart feels so peaceful and exhilarated all at the same time? As you worship me, you put yourself in a position to receive all the amazing gifts I have for you. It is difficult to accept what I offer when your arms are full.

Come away with me. Just for a while. Sit and soak up my splendor. Breathe in my beauty.

I love you,
Abba

My Abba,

Thank you for this invitation to worship you. Thank you for asking me to enjoy a daily furlough in the most glorious place in all the universe — past, present, and future — the sanctuary of your presence.

When I bow before you, you bring my heart into delightful admiration. I enjoy who you are (and who I am through you) as I savor the endless, iridescent waters of your matchless grace. Wave after wave washing over me.

"I will return without jet lag, missing luggage, or a sunburn. How can I lose?"

Sometimes I am overwhelmed and weep. Sometimes I smile. Sometimes I am challenged. Sometimes I simply rest. But when I get a glimpse of your beauty inviting my heart into your glorious respite, I am never left earthbound.

Transform me again with the magnificent light of your love. My heart, mind and body will be renewed. And I will return without jet lag, missing luggage, or a sunburn. How can I lose?

I love you,
Mollie

EMERGING LOVE

"And you must love the Lord
your God with all your heart,
all your soul, all your mind,
and all your strength." MARK 12:30

My Abba,

I realize my intense feeling of deep affection for you is so diminutive compared with the love for you I will eventually enjoy. But I am in awe of what I have experienced so far. Thank you for supernaturally seeding that love in my heart.

I see "Love the Lord your God" is a constant refrain in Scripture. My immediate response when I read it is, "Of course, I love you. To know you is to love you." Then I really consider the meanings of the words in this verse. And I feel as confident as my five-year-old self peering over the end of the high diving board at the swimming pool.

There is a lot of space between me and where I want to be.

I want my priorities to testify to your matchless value, importance and worth. I want to clearly show my respect and admiration for you. I want to live to appreciate and reflect your utter relevance. I want to be faithful to you — loyal and steadfast. I want to delight in you.

Are my heart, soul, mind and strength captivated by you? Are my feelings, impulses, affections, and desires fueled by my passion for you? Is my love such that my very life is devoted to you? Are my intentions, thoughts, intellect and understanding focused on you?

---

*ABBA: a personal name for father that implies warm affectio
LOVE: (agapa)* value, esteem, feel or manifest generous concern for, be faithful towards, to delight in   HEART: (kardia)* regarded as the seat of feeling, impulse, affection, desire   SOUL: (psyche)* the seat of religious and moral sentiment   MIND: (dianoia)* thought, intention, intellect, understanding.   STRENGTH: (ischus)* strength, might, power, faculty, ability   *definitions from Greek n and devoted trust.*

Is all my strength, might, power, and ability aimed at pursuing relationship with you?

I am obviously still a novice in my love for you, even after all these years. Please continue to grow my love for you and all that is important to you.

I love you,
Mollie

My Child,

Your love for me brings me joy. Even though it is not unwavering, fully formed, or perfectly expressed. I see the desires of your heart, and I am always working to grow you up.

Think of one of your grandsons expressing his love by bringing you a single wilted flower, a special crayon drawing, or a clay sculpture. How do you feel when he calls your name, runs to you, and throws his arms around you? His love is young. He does not communicate it in sophisticated ways, but it delights your heart. I feel that way about you.

> *"I want a love relationship with you so profound it is contagious."*

I want the outward expression of your love for me to result in others desiring a deeper connection with me. I want more than just a bond with you through your knowledge of the truth. I want a love relationship with you so profound it is contagious.

Hollywood depicts human romance in a way that makes everyone want what is on the big screen. (A longing is fed for that perfect man or woman with whom you will live happily ever after.) Unfortunately, the love stories they script are fantasy. The best romance between two people will never satisfy the longing I created in you just for me. Forever love with me is an attainable reality that is eternally satisfying.

As you walk with me, you will carry the life-giving fragrance of being in relationship with me. This is not fantasy. You will thrive in my embrace.

I love you,
Abba

FRAGRANT DAYS

"Therefore, six days before the Passover, Jesus came to Bethany where Lazarus was, whom Jesus had raised from the dead. So they made Him a dinner there, and Martha was serving; and Lazarus was one of those reclining at the table with Him. Mary then took a pound of very expensive perfume of pure nard, and anointed the feet of Jesus and wiped His feet with her hair; and the house was filled with the fragrance of the perfume." JOHN 12:1–3

My Abba,

I really don't know how to express myself right now. This morning, your beauty overwhelms me. You disarm all the pain, confusion, fatigue, failure, and disappointment that needles my heart.

I know you are always with me. But when you open my heart to notice you in a deeper way, it makes me insatiable for your presence.

You set this feast before me. I have tasted and seen that your love is better than life. I do not want to forget. Make my hunger for you consuming. Just to enjoy a small taste of your presence is delightful. Please draw me back again and again.

I want you to extravagantly nourish our connection. I want to spend myself on this forever love. Empower me to pour out the perfume of my praise before you. Fill my life with the captivating fragrance of our relationship, my beautiful God.

I love you,
Mollie

My Child,

I love that you are drawn to this account of Mary's sacrificial devotion. Even though her actions were costly and utterly humbling, it was well worth it to her. She was willing to devote her life to the One who gave her life and would continue to enliven her.

When soldiers go into battle, they are not as apt to make sacrifices for their superiors and country, if they are just compelled by the duty of "shoulds" and "ought to's." But a deep devotion for their commander, fellow soldiers, or country will inspire heroic acts.

> *"As you steep in my love, your service will become the lingering fragrance of our connection."*

You want to live in devotion to me because of who I am. An ever-deepening connection with me is worth everything. Our relationship will inspire you to live for me courageously. I know you can be distracted at times, but your heart is toward me. Don't get fixated on serving, like Martha did, and miss the glorious excitement and mystery of our love.

Allow me to permeate every corner of your heart. You will never go away dissatisfied. I am the God who satisfies needs you don't even know you have. Sit and soak in me. Then serve. As you steep in my love, your service will become the lingering fragrance of our connection.

I love you,
Abba

ABOUT THE AUTHOR

Mollie Axtell delights in her ever-deepening relationship with Christ. She believes her greatest strength is her dependence on God. Mollie has enjoyed teaching God's Word for over four decades and has led a Celebrate Recovery group in Austin for the last nine years. She feels most alive when worshiping, writing, teaching and swimming in Texas Hill Country lakes. Mollie has been married for over 43 years and has three children and three grandchildren.

ACKNOWLEDGMENTS

Cal, my husband for over 43 years who not only cooked for me while I wrote, but edited for me afterwards

Brooke, my fierce daughter "made of eyes" who inspired me to pick up the pen

Erin, my ever-encouraging baby sister who kept me going when I desperately wanted to give up

Tamara, my talented book designer whose patience and creativity are boundless

Bean, my blonde soul twin who understands me, even when I may not understand myself

PHOTO CREDITS

All photos © [photographer's name listed]/123RF.com unless otherwise noted.

Copyright page: t.fikar
Introduction: ammentorp
Abba's Child: e.koifman
Making a Masterpiece: jpchret
No Fairy Tale: paut-fluerasu
Fully Known. Fully Loved.: t.tomsickova
Treasured: anna-marie west (also p. 1)
Threadbare Beauty: potowizard
Child of Promise: kavram
Passion to Please: tatiana kostareva
No Strut or Grovel: manganganath
Currency of Desire: sritongcom
Extreme Makeover: hanohiki
Diabolical, Delusional, or Divine: choate
Holding the Universe and Me: miloszg
Skywriting: mihajlovic (also p. 31)
Marvelous or Maniacal: p.jauhiainen
Worshiping the Giver: g.santa maria
Mercy to Breathe: anyaberkut
Something From Nothing: g.andrushko
Pride in My Glory: d.jacobsen
Courage to Speak: realstock
Waiting Well: soloway
Brave Enough: byrdyak (also p. 59)
Soothing My Soul: a.mayovskyy
Surprising Superheroes: k.carden
Obsessed With My Prize: ivan kruk
Real Life: k.carden
Longing for Light: zhuralov
Captive Gaze: silkstocking
Relaxing Clenched Fists: stillfx
Neon Lights: fei wong
Glimmer in the Dark: i.zhuravlov (also p. 75)
Strong Medicine: e.schweitzer
Better Than Life: d.pichugin
Life Support: goncharenko (also p. 97)

Be My Rescue: mihtiander
Promise Keeper: rustyphil
My Remedy: a.rath
Inseparable: a.amat
Fooling Ourselves: v.stuchelova
Read My Lips: lassedesignen
Shifting Shadows & Heavenly Lights: i.zhuravlov (also p. 119)
The Art of Remaining: j.chalabala
A Confident Approach: e.pimenov
Every Moment of Forever: zhuravlov
Unbridled Bliss, p. 139: atamanenko
Thunder and Whisper: kevin carden
The Party Never Ends: solarseven
Oasis: j.vitanovski
Waking to Wonder: dyed4youart
See and Be Glad: konstanttin
Unbridled Bliss: personal photo by Sarah Garza
What Are You Drinking?: m. pelin
At Home: m.gorbunov
Living Love: s. tryapitsyn
Power to Cling: atamanenko
The Kindness of Conviction: nejron (also p. 157)
God's Green Thumb: v.chursina
Love Laws: lightwise
Limping Home: rdonar
Savor the Sip: anna om
Exposed Thorns: janroz (also p. 181)
Pools of Blessing: p. opaska
Swimming With Alligators: p.durieu
Life in the Briar Patch: j.holcombe
Making Monet: chertok
Was it Because…: w.kertchot
Defy the Darkness: k.carden
Cracked Clay: Deviant Art, danchristopher
Seeing Through Doubt: n. standret
Captivated: t.tomsickova

In The Labyrinth: gordond (also p. 213)
Your Road, Reality, and Roots: boule13
Overflowing Hope: tomas1111
Honeysuckle on the Wind: e.sergeev
One of Those: blasbike
Dry Up, Blow Up, or Grow Up: sudthangtum
Treasure Trove: r.tavani
Rabbit Holes and Reality: e.schweitzer (also p. 231)
Identity Truth: i.chiosea
Wisdom From Above: personal photo
Prayerful and Proactive: gracel21
Making Me Rich: r.mayer
Bags of Gold: b.wylezich
The Moment He Knocks: horoshevych
Gifts For My Enemies: michal bednarek
Promised to Your Path: zflzf (also p. 247)
Strike a Chord: studio 3321
Superfood: kurhan
Make Us One: rawpixel (also p. 267)
Difficult Ones: siriburanakit
Ignite Our Souls: dolgachov
Love With Legs: tryapitsyn
Caught Up In Your Symphony: pixelrobot
Unveiled: khomiakov
With or Without Words: anyka
Come On In: ammentorp
Deep Roots: vilanova
One Thing: mikhail laptev
Staycation: p.koch
Emerging Love: personal photo
Fragrant Days: z.ivanova (also p. 289)
Page 312: alinamd
About the Author: personal photo

www.ingramcontent.com/pod-product-compliance
Lightning Source LLC
Chambersburg PA
CBHW070042120526
44589CB00035B/2085